I AM FEARFULLY AND WONDERFULLY MADE [Psalm 139:14] – I praise you, for I am fearfully and w[...] my soul knows it very well. I AM FILLED WITH JOY [John 17:13] – But now I am coming to you, [...] they may have my joy fulfilled in themselves. I AM BEING COMPLETED [Philippians 1:6] – And I am [...] in you will bring it to completion at the day of Jesus Christ. I AM CLEANSED [1 John 1:9] – If w[...] forgive us our sins and to cleanse us from all unrighteousness. I AM COMPLETE IN CHRIST [Coloss[...] through your union with Christ, who is the head over every ruler and authority. I AM ABLE [Philip[...] who strengthens me. I AM ALIVE [Ephesians 2:4-5] – But God, being rich in mercy, because of [...] when we were dead in our trespasses, made us alive together with Christ – by grace you have [...] But God's firm foundation stands, bearing this seal: "The Lord knows those who are his," and, "Let everyone who names the name of the [Lo]rd depart from iniquity." I AM FILLED WITH THE KNOWLEDGE OF HIS WILL [Colossians 1:9-10] – And so, from the day we heard, we have not [ce]ased to pray for you, asking that you may be filled with the knowledge of his will in all spiritual wisdom and understanding, so as to walk [i]n a manner worthy of the Lord, fully pleasing to him, bearing fruit in every good work and increasing in the knowledge of God. I AM FILLED [WI]TH THE FRUIT OF THE SPIRIT [Galatians 5:22-23 (NLT)] – But the Holy Spirit produces this kind of fruit in our lives: love, joy, peace, patience, kindness, goodness, faithfulness, gentleness, and self-control. There is no law against these things! I AM DRAWING NEAR WITH CONFIDENCE [Hebrews 4:16] – Let us then with confidence draw near to the throne of grace, that we may receive mercy and find grace to help in time of need. I AM IN CHRIST [1 Corinthians 1:30-31] – You are in Christ Jesus, who became to us wisdom from God, righteousness and sanctification and redemption, so that, as it is written, "Let the one who boasts, boast in the Lord." I AM INCLUDED [Ephesians 1:13-14] – And you also were included in Christ when you heard the message of truth, the gospel of your salvation. When you believed, you were marked in him with a seal, the promised Holy Spirit, who is a deposit guaranteeing our inheritance until the redemption of those who are God's possession – to the praise of his glory. I AM HIDDEN WITH CHRIST IN GOD [Colossians 3:3] – For you have died, and your life is hidden with Christ in God. I AM HIS HANDIWORK [Ephesians 2:10 (NIV)] – For we are God's handiwork, created in Christ Jesus to do good works, which God prepared in advance for us to do. I AM HEALED [1 Peter 2:24] – He himself bore our sins in his body on the tree, that we might die to sin and live to righteousness. By his wounds you have been healed. I AM AN HEIR [Titus 3:7] – So that being justified by his grace we might become heirs according to the hope of eternal life. I AM FORGIVEN [Ephesians 1:7 (NLT)] – He is so rich in kindness and grace that he purchased our freedom with the blood of his Son and forgave our sins. I AM A CO-HEIR WITH CHRIST [Romans 8:17 (NIV)] – Now if we are children, then we are heirs – heirs of God and co-heirs with Christ, if indeed we share in his sufferings in order that we may also share in his glory. I AM COMFORTED [Jeremiah 31:13 (NIV)] – Then young women will dance and be glad, young men and old as well. I will turn their mourning into gladness; I will give them comfort and joy instead of sorrow. I AM CONFIDENT [1 John 4:17] – By this is love perfected with us, so that we may have confidence for the day of judgement, because as he is so also are we in this world. I AM BOLD [Proverbs 28:1 (NLT)] – The wicked flee when no one pursues, but the righteous are bold as a lion. I AM ACCEPTED [Ephesians 1:4-6] – Even as he chose us in him before the foundation of the world, that we should be holy and blameless before him. In love he predestined us for adoption as sons through Jesus Christ, according to the purpose of his will, to the praise of his glorious grace, with which he has blessed us in the Beloved. I AM ADEQUATE [2 Corinthians 3:5 (AMP)] Not that we are sufficiently qualified in ourselves to claim anything as coming from us, but our sufficiency and qualifications come from God. I AM ABRAHAM'S OFFSPRING [Galatians 3:29] – And if you are Christ's, then you are Abraham's offspring, heirs according to promise. I AM ANXIOUS FOR NOTHING [Philippians 4:6-7] – Do not be anxious about anything, but in everything by prayer and supplication with thanksgiving let your requests be made known to God. And the peace of God, which surpasses all understanding, will guard your hearts and your minds in Christ Jesus. I AM BORN AGAIN [1 Peter 1:23 (NIV)] – For you have been born again, not of perishable seed, but of imperishable, through the living and enduring word of God. I AM BOUGHT WITH A PRICE [1 Corinthians 6:20] – For you were bought with a price. So glorify God in your body. I AM A BRANCH OF THE TRUE VINE [John 15:5] – I am the vine; you are the branches. Whoever abides in me and I in him, he it is that bears much fruit, for apart from me you can do nothing. I AM CLAY IN THE POTTER'S HAND [Jeremiah 18:6] – O house of Israel, can I not do with you as this potter has done? declares the Lord. Behold, like the clay in the potter's hand, so are you in my hand, O house of Israel. I AM CLEAN [John 15:3] – Already you are clean because of the word that I have spoken to you. I AM CREATED IN HIS IMAGE [Genesis 1:27] – So God created man in his own image, in the image of God he created him; male and female he created them. I AM COURAGEOUS [1 Chronicles 28:20] – Then David said to Solomon his son, "Be strong and courageous and do it. Do not be afraid and do not be dismayed, for the Lord God, even my God, is with you. He will not leave you or forsake you, until all the work for the service of the house of the Lord is finished." I AM CRUCIFIED WITH HIM [Galatians 2:20] – I have been crucified with Christ. It is no longer I who live, but Christ who lives in me. And the life I now live in the flesh I live by faith in the Son of God, who loved me and gave himself for me. I AM DEAD IN CHRIST [Romans 6:4] – We were buried therefore with him by baptism into death, in order that, just as Christ was raised from the dead by the glory of the Father, we too might walk in newness of life. I AM HIS DELIGHT [Psalm 147:11(NIV)] – The Lord delights in those who fear him, who put their hope in his unfailing love. I AM EMPOWERED TO OBEY [Philippians 2:13 (NIV)] For it is God who works in you to will and to act in order to fulfil his good purpose. I AM ENCOURAGED [2 Thessalonians 2:16-17] – May our Lord Jesus Christ himself and God our Father, who loved us and by his grace gave us eternal encouragement and good hope, encourage your hearts and strengthen you in every good deed and word. I AM ENLIGHTENED [Ephesians 1:18 (NIV)] – I pray that the eyes of your heart may be enlightened in order that you may know the hope to which he has called you, the riches of his glorious inheritance in his holy people. I AM ADOPTED [Ephesians 1:5 (NIV)] – He predestined us to be adopted as his sons through Jesus Christ, in accordance with his pleasure and will. I AM AN AMBASSADOR FOR CHRIST [2 Corinthians 5:20] – Therefore, we are ambassadors for Christ, God making his appeal through us. We implore you on behalf of Christ, be reconciled to God. I AM ASSURED SUCCESS [Proverbs 16:3 (AMP)] – Commit your works to the Lord [submit and trust them to Him], and your plans will succeed [if you respond to his will and guidance]. I AM CONFIDENT THAT HE WILL NEVER LEAVE ME [Hebrews 13:5-6] – Keep your life free from love of money, and be content with what you have, for he has said, "I will never leave you nor forsake you." So we can confidently say, "The Lord is my helper; I will not fear; what can man do to me?" I AM CONTENT [Philippians 4:11] Not that I am speaking of being in need, for I have learned in whatever situation I am to be content. I AM DEAD TO SIN [Romans 6:11] – So you also must consider yourselves dead to sin and alive to God in Christ Jesus.

FOR YOU FORMED MY INWARD PARTS; YOU KNITTED ME TOGETHER IN MY MOTHER'S WOMB. I PRAISE YOU, FOR I AM FEARFULLY AND WONDERFULLY

MADE.

PSALM 139:13 (ESV)

"GOD

KNOWS OUR REAL IDENTITY. GOD HAS DESIGNED YOU IN A SPECIFIC WAY TO BE YOU. YOU WILL ALWAYS BE A BAD COPY OF SOMEONE ELSE, BUT ONLY YOU CAN BE THE BEST YOU."

DAN WATSON

FIRST PUBLISHED IN GREAT BRITAIN IN 2019

SOCIETY FOR PROMOTING CHRISTIAN KNOWLEDGE
36 CAUSTON STREET
LONDON SW1P 4ST
WWW.SPCK.ORG.UK

FOR CREDITS AND COPYRIGHT ACKNOWLEDGEMENTS, SEE P.223

BRITISH LIBRARY CATALOGUING-IN-PUBLICATION DATA
A CATALOGUE RECORD FOR THIS BOOK IS AVAILABLE FROM THE BRITISH LIBRARY

ISBN 978-0-281-07864-6
EBOOK ISBN 978-0-281-07865-3

1 3 5 7 9 10 8 6 4 2

DESIGNED AND TYPESET BY ABRUPT MEDIA
FIRST PRINTED IN TURKEY BY ELMA BASIM YAYIN VE ILETISIM HIZMETLERI SAN. TIC. LTD. STI.

ABRUPT MEDIA

FEARFULLY MADE

YOUTH X YOUNG ADULTS

POSITIVELY SHAPING SOCIETY

FEARFULLY **MADE** CONTENTS

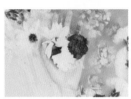

**"DO NOT BE AFRAID; DO NOT BE DISCOURAGED,
FOR THE LORD YOUR GOD WILL BE WITH YOU
WHEREVER YOU GO."**

JOSHUA 1:9 (NIV)

FEARFULLY **MADE** CONTENTS
POSITIVELY SHAPING SOCIETY

"THE LORD IS WITH ME; I WILL NOT BE AFRAID. WHAT CAN MERE MORTALS DO TO ME?"
PSALM 118:6 (NIV)

"IN THAT MOMENT, I FELT AN OVERWHELMING PEACE SURROUND ME, A PEACE THAT ASSURED ME THAT GOD HAD GOOD PLANS FOR ME."
CARINE HARB

BUT DON'T MISUNDERSTAND: YOU DON'T REALLY NEED TO BE AFRAID OF GOD, BECAUSE GOD CARES FOR EVERY LITTLE SPARROW. HOW MUCH IS A SPARROW WORTH — DON'T FIVE OF THEM SELL FOR A FEW CENTS? SINCE YOU ARE SO MUCH MORE PRECIOUS TO GOD THAN A THOUSAND FLOCKS OF SPARROWS, AND SINCE GOD KNOWS YOU IN EVERY DETAIL — DOWN TO THE NUMBER OF HAIRS ON YOUR HEAD AT THIS MOMENT — YOU CAN BE SECURE AND UNAFRAID OF ANY PERSON, AND YOU HAVE NOTHING TO FEAR FROM GOD EITHER.

LUKE 12:6-7 (THE VOICE)

FEARFULLY
MADE

BY: DAN WATSON

ur society has an identity issue. People are searching for who they are. We look to our peers, to social media, to Hollywood, to find out who we should be. But God knows our real identity. He says we are 'fearfully and wonderfully made.'

Reading through, that's what this book is all about: understanding who has made us and who he has made us to be. Understanding that there are fears that tell us we shouldn't, or we mustn't, or we can't live fearlessly out of this God-given identity.

Fear affects us all. For me, the fear of rejection in my life was huge. Doesn't everyone just want to be 'normal'? I often felt like if I were ever to do something or say something that stood out I would be rejected. And so, I held back or conformed, just wanting to fit in. That's when my fear of loneliness kicked in too. Whether isolated or surrounded by loads of people, it can feel so lonely to not be yourself or have your true self be known.

At times it can feel like we're the only one who feels this way, but what I love about this book is that it shows us we're not alone. The stories and interviews in this book are shared to show you are not alone in your fear but with God you can, and you will, overcome it.

Singer-songwriter Fleur East tells us about her fear of failure when taking to the stage in *The X Factor*, and Guvna B shares his struggle to fit in and how he found his true voice. Designer Marcel tells us about overcoming the fear of ridicule, with singer-songwriter Leah McFall encouraging us all to 'absolutely know the word of God so we're well equipped to deal with these lies and these fears that are spoken over us.'

Broadcaster Ashley John-Baptiste, shares with us how God changed his fear of rejection, with preacher Rich Wilkerson JR encouraging us to face fear head on. Cheryl Fagan delves into the fear of loneliness and how it is only God who can satisfy, and church leader Chelsea Smith encourages us with her promise that she 'would never say no to anything God asked her to do because of fear'.

Born in Lebanon, Carine Harb shares how God helped her overcome her very real fear of death, with Erwin McManus challenging us that 'fear is the baseline to the next great breakthrough in your life'. All of these fears and all of these interviews point to the one fear that can conquer them all, with Designer William Adoasi and church leader Lucille Houston further unpacking how the fear of God can overcome all other fears.

These features and so many more packed into this book, encourage us that if we understand that we are fearfully and wonderfully made, we can step out of everything society has boxed us into. As I share myself, if I was to listen to what society said about my life I would just be another negative statistic. I would not have the marriage I have, be the father I am or be able to do what I do now. But once I listened to what God says and understand that I'm made in his image, he gave me the power to change my narrative. That doesn't mean I don't get scared – we all do – but it means I don't let fear have a grip on me so that each day I can step out into all he has for me.

This book is for everyone but specifically for a young person or leader who is trying to navigate their identity in life, trying to understand who Jesus is and how he has made us unique, that we can all be used for a purpose and fight for a common goal which is to point more and more people to him.

My hope is that this book will help all readers step out of a place of fear and step into their God-given potential, their full purpose in positively shaping society. I pray you would be inspired to just be yourself, understanding that God has designed you in a specific way to be you. You will always be a bad copy of someone else, but only you can be the best you. So, go live your best life.

CHAPTER 1 FEAR OF FAILURE

"NEVER DOUBT GOD'S MIGHTY POWER TO WORK IN YOU AND ACCOMPLISH ALL THIS. HE WILL ACHIEVE INFINITELY MORE THAN YOUR GREATEST REQUEST, YOUR MOST UNBELIEVABLE DREAM, AND EXCEED YOUR WILDEST IMAGINATION! HE WILL OUTDO THEM ALL, FOR HIS MIRACULOUS POWER CONSTANTLY ENERGIZES YOU." EPHESIANS 3:20 (TPT)

FEAR OF
FAILURE

FAILURE. THERE IS SUCH A STIGMA ATTACHED TO THIS WORD, ONE THAT SUGGESTS MISTAKE, REGRET, GUILT, ANXIETY AND FEAR. WE BECOME AFRAID OF FAILING BECAUSE OF THE STIGMA ATTACHED. WHAT WILL OTHERS THINK OF ME? WHAT IF I TRY AGAIN AND FAIL? THE QUESTIONS CIRCULATE AROUND OUR MINDS AND CONTRIBUTE TO THE RISING FEAR.

BY: JO WATSON

Within our society, perfection, qualification and the number of people wanting to observe your life are often viewed as success and achieve recognition. You're doing the right thing, 'winning at life', 'living your best life'.

This fear of failing so often prevents people from stepping out and achieving the dreams or goals they may have. We become so fearful we don't even allow ourselves to speak out about what we're imagining might happen. We're isolated in the fear that we may fail and as a result be rejected or humiliated.

Fear of failure is rife within society. All you need to do is visit a school or university and earwig into a conversation to hear the commonly heard phrase, 'There's no point me even trying, I'll only get it wrong,' or sit in a parents' group and listen as they anxiously discuss their children's potential failures to meet specific milestones. We are bombarded with society's criteria as to what our lives should look like at more or less every age, and when we don't appear to be matching up, the fear of failure has the potential to increase and rear its ugly head.

For me personally, the fear of failure has been and continues to be something I regularly have to overcome. There have been so many times in the past when I have allowed the fear to rule my decisions, and therefore hold me back from opportunities, because ultimately I did not have the confidence or belief to overcome it. A time that I often recall is when I first went to university at the age of twenty. Within the first two weeks, everyone had to take a 'diagnostic test' to check our ability levels. Not long after having our papers marked, I received mine back with the dreaded words 'See me' on. See me! It's always in red too as if those two words together aren't enough on their own. I remember at that point questioning my ability to carry on with the course, but I thought it was too soon and again, because of the fear of what people would say, I decided to stick it out. I was soon diagnosed with dyslexia and heard phrases such as, 'We're surprised you did as well as you did in school.' But I can't say it was all bad; it did mean I was given extra time when it came to exams!

For me, this fear only grew stronger during my time at university and reached a peak during one of my placements, resulting in me making the decision to leave the course. I was so overwhelmed with the fear of failing my assignments, observations and ultimately the course, and as mentioned previously, I just didn't have the confidence or belief to overcome it.

Being a Christian since the age of sixteen I was aware of what the Bible said and

> "WE ARE BOMBARDED WITH SOCIETY'S CRITERIA AS TO WHAT OUR LIVES SHOULD LOOK LIKE AT MORE OR LESS EVERY AGE, AND WHEN WE DON'T APPEAR TO BE MATCHING UP, THE FEAR OF FAILURE HAS THE POTENTIAL TO INCREASE AND REAR ITS UGLY HEAD."

"GRACE IS THE POWER TO BELIEVE THAT WHAT GOD SAYS IS TRUE BUT ALSO TO MOVE ON AND GO AGAIN WHEN THERE ARE TIMES WHERE THINGS DON'T GO TO PLAN OR WE FEEL LIKE WE'VE MISSED IT. GRACE IS KEY, AND THE BIBLE TELLS US THAT GOD'S GRACE IS SUFFICIENT, MEANING ENOUGH. IT'S ENOUGH FOR US."

could quote verses such as, 'I can do all things through Christ who strengthens me,' but I don't think I truly had a revelation of what it meant or looked like for me in my everyday life. I had little confidence in myself and my own ability to achieve academically, as I'd often struggled throughout my school years and frequently required extra support. I had been considered to be 'average' or only just hitting the mark in the major subjects.

For me, as I said earlier, this is an area I constantly have to allow God to rule over and speak into. It has taken time to develop a belief and confidence now that is not solely in me but in God and who he says I am. As I found out more about God and what he has to say in this area, I was able to return to university a few years later with a completely different approach and mind-set. That doesn't mean I was completely fearless, but the difference was I was able to overcome it by allowing God to overrule. For example, the thought of having to write a 10,000-word dissertation for me was not just daunting but almost like a huge sign being held up in front of me saying, 'This is impossible for you.' Every time I would sit down to write, my default thought was, 'You can't do this.' It took time and discipline to actually train my mind to think differently. There's a verse in the Bible that speaks about allowing God to renew your mind (Romans 12:2), and that's literally what I have to regularly do: ask God to identify thoughts that are not true and show me his truth. I have learnt to hold on to his word and when I feel like backing out or giving up, I ask myself, 'Is it because I'm scared to fail?' Nine times out of ten it is.

In my life, I know that without my faith in God, in who he is and who he says I am, the daily battle with fear of failure often results in 1–0 to fear. However, what I have learnt is that God's word tells me I'm accepted whether I match up to criteria or not. He has a plan for me. He has equipped me, given me the mind of Christ and, as if that wasn't enough, gone before me. Additionally, the icing on the cake if you like, there is his grace. I often thought of grace as forgiveness alone but over the years and through various challenges I've come to know grace as power. Grace is the power to believe that what God says is true but also to move on and go again when there are times where things don't go to plan or we feel like we've missed it. Grace is key, and the Bible tells us that God's grace is sufficient, meaning enough. It's enough for us.

So when the fear of failure tries to consume me, I just allow the grace of God to overpower it by speaking out his truth.

JO WATSON pastors the Youth & Young Adults of Hillsong UK along with her husband, Dan. She is mum to two beautiful children Isabella East & Jude Jenson. Originally from the north of England in Lancashire, Jo moved to London at the age of 19 and fell in love with the city. As a qualified Social Worker, Jo has a real passion for people and creating opportunities for those who wouldn't normally be provided them.

HOW BLESSED IS GOD!

AND WHAT A BLESSING HE IS! HE'S THE FATHER OF OUR MASTER, JESUS CHRIST, AND TAKES US TO THE HIGH PLACES OF BLESSING IN HIM. LONG BEFORE HE LAID DOWN EARTH'S FOUNDATIONS, HE HAD US IN MIND, HAD SETTLED ON US AS THE FOCUS OF HIS LOVE, TO BE MADE WHOLE AND HOLY BY HIS LOVE. LONG, LONG AGO HE DECIDED TO ADOPT US INTO HIS FAMILY THROUGH JESUS CHRIST. (WHAT PLEASURE HE TOOK IN PLANNING THIS!) HE WANTED US TO ENTER INTO THE CELEBRATION OF HIS LAVISH GIFT-GIVING BY THE HAND OF HIS BELOVED SON.

EPHESIANS 1:3-6 (MSG)

DANIEL
FEODOROFF

POSITIVELY SHAPING SOCIETY X SYDNEY

HILLSONG YOUTH X YOUNG ADULTS

FEAR OF FAILURE

"EVERY NIGHT I WOULD JUMP FROM MY BED JUST TO AVOID THE MONSTER UNDERNEATH. TURNS OUT NOTHING WAS THERE!"

Where were you born?
Sydney, Australia

What do you do?
I'm currently studying at university for a Bachelor of Industrial Design.

What hobbies do you have?
I like design and technology.

Who inspires you to be fearless and why?
God inspires me to be fearless because through him I know that anything to glorify him is possible.

What were you scared of as a child?
To be honest it was the 'monster' under my bed. Every night I would jump from my bed just to avoid the monster underneath. Turns out nothing was there!

What's the biggest risk you've taken?
Starting two businesses, one Business IT service helping businesses run their digital lives better and a Smart Home Automation business to help everyday families get their homes connected to their phones and Siri.

Do you have a key verse you live by to overcome fear?
2 Timothy 1:7. 'The Spirit God gave us does not make us afraid. His Spirit is a source of power and love and self-control.'

Do you have a favourite book that's helped you on your spiritual journey?
Unstoppable by Christine Caine was given to me by a special friend at A21 when I was doing charity work for them. It showed me just how fearless to be under God and helped me realize how much the world really needs help through God.

What do you think about hope in today's culture that tells us to put our hope in things like fame, fortune, success? Today's culture is so focused in the materialistic items that they forget what they are made for. Current society is obsessive and compulsive, replacing religion with partying, getting drunk, sex and other things. Many people tell us that we don't need Jesus to be happy. All we need is to have a good time. At school everyone tells us that if we don't do well we will fail and go nowhere, but if you put faith in Jesus it's a completely different story, as he gives us direction and purpose.

How has your relationship with Jesus redefined how you view and overcome fear? Jesus has completely changed the way I deal with fear and failure. I know in tough times I can put my faith in him and I will get through it. When going through tough times like exams and it feels like you just suck and you're crying for days because you feel like you're a failure, I just remember that God has a plan for me and pray to get through this with God on top.

Fear of God, means that we stand in awe, in wonder of him. What do you think is powerful and important about remembering the greatness and goodness of God? What's powerful and important about God is he has a plan and a purpose for your life. He has mapped your future out before you were born and he is just waiting for you to unlock it with your faith. He doesn't care when you stuff up. He only cares about loving you and leading you on your path.

Where do you feel God is leading you in the future? Through the two businesses I run I have learnt that I have a gift in communication and strategic thinking. These skills have led me to places that I could only dream of and it's been such a blessing in my life. Recently God has blessed me by opening doors in my life through connections, such as being able to meet with Apple to

"HE DOESN'T CARE WHEN YOU STUFF UP. HE ONLY CARES ABOUT LOVING YOU AND LEADING YOU ON YOUR PATH."

talk about my ideas, being able to go to China on a business trip with a client and being able to work with companies to create better apps for their customers.

I feel God has made me an entrepreneur for a reason which I am still unpacking and realizing throughout my walk.

What advice would you give the next generation, wanting to follow a dream but feeling fearful? If you gave them all a personal message what would you say? God has given you a unique talent that he wants to use within you and turn into something amazing.

Pray about it and press into it with your faith. This can really help with understanding where God wants you to go. Also, remain open to what other people have to say because sometimes things you want to do or think you're good at can be distractions from the path God really wants you to take.

What's one area in your life that you've felt the fear of failure? What happened? School has always been hard for me as I have never been a star student getting loads of As. I've never really liked school as it constricts my passions and doesn't let me grow in my

abilities. I am passionate about design and it's the only class at school that I am good at. One of my teachers said to me earlier in the year that she thinks I will fail school, uni and in life in general.

When it comes to exams I study and put in the work but for some reason never do well. It's been a very hard time in my life as constantly falling short of your expectations is emotionally draining. After exams and getting results back I normally curl up in a ball and cry for days about how bad I feel. I've had so many successes over the past couple of years but I still feel like a failure to myself and to my parents as I am scared about the marks I will be getting at the end.

Thankfully, I have now learnt how to deal with these times and feel okay. Firstly, God helps me through these times. Just a simple prayer asking for peace at heart and in soul can help me feel a thousand times better. I always know that God is there as whenever I feel down or like a failure he always shines his light into the situation, making me realize that this is not the ultimate defining moment in my life. This has ultimately changed the way I view this whole situation

as there is no need to worry, because God has created a plan and a purpose for my life, and if school isn't something that I'm gifted at, then I guess he doesn't want me to worry about it but find the stuff that I am good at, like business.

Hillsong Youth has been so important to me over the past few years as it's helped me understand my calling and helped me to grow closer to God. During my early years in high school I didn't think much about Youth and never really attended. Now I've realized how important it is in the development of my faith, I never want to miss a week for anything. When I stand amongst everyone worshiping, my worries, fears and failures wash away as I understand how God wants me to feel, which is loved and accepted just as I am.

Throughout my school life, my faith has been challenged and there have been times where I've felt God has not been there for me, but in reality he was just working on the bigger picture and was waiting for me to step right into his plan for me.

Overall, my faith has been strengthened and I've never felt closer to God than I do right now.

"THROUGHOUT MY SCHOOL LIFE, MY FAITH HAS BEEN CHALLENGED AND THERE HAVE BEEN TIMES WHERE I'VE FELT GOD HAS NOT BEEN THERE FOR ME, BUT IN REALITY HE WAS JUST WORKING ON THE BIGGER PICTURE AND WAS WAITING FOR ME TO STEP RIGHT INTO HIS PLAN FOR ME."

FLEUR
EAST

"Have faith that God only wants to guide you in a direction that is good for you and he will be with you every step of the way."

FEAR OF FAILURE

HE WILL COVER YOU WITH HIS
FEATHERS, AND UNDER HIS
WINGS YOU WILL FIND REFUGE;
HIS FAITHFULNESS WILL BE
YOUR SHIELD AND RAMPART.

PSALM 91:4 (NIV)

WHO INSPIRES YOU TO BE FEARLESS AND WHY?

My mum. Definitely. My mum is like my prayer pillar - she has always been a devout Christian, taking us to church, teaching us how to pray. I feel safe because I know I've got her. She's been through a lot in life, and she's always been fearless, because she has so much faith in God.

What were you scared of as a child? Did you have any particular fears? Oh my gosh! I was the biggest scared-y cat. I was scared of everything. In some ways I think because I was introduced to God so early on, I also knew about the devil – good and evil – from a really early age.

I remember this one dream I had when I was eight so vividly. I was standing at the altar and was asked to recite the Lord's Prayer and I opened my mouth and I just couldn't.

I woke up crying my eyes out and my mum came into the room and said, 'Listen, don't let this scare you. Let's just say it together.'

So we both said the Lord's Prayer together.

What do you think is the biggest risk you've taken? I think one was definitely going on The *X Factor*. I had been on it when I was younger in a girl group so I had already experienced the show, but we only went to the live show for one week before being kicked out – so I only got a taste. Then I toured as part of DJ Fresh's band, but I was always in the background. So going on the show alone and being forced into the spotlight was a big risk for me.

Have you got a key verse you live by? Definitely. What my mum says: I can do anything through Christ who strengthens me, and Christ has shown that to me. That is something that I definitely live by. But my mum has always taught me to read Psalm 91 before I go to bed, and one line that always comforts me is: 'He will cover you with his feathers, and under his wings you will find refuge.'

So looking at today's culture, there are certain expectations regarding looks, relationships, education that we are all operating under. What do you think are the key pressures facing young people today? I imagine you get asked advice on how to handle these a lot? Yeah. I always get asked for advice, mostly questions about my job like, 'How do I stay focused?' and 'How do I try not to compete with others?' The majority of young people today are on social media and flooded with stories of successful people and thinking, 'How can I live up to that?' My advice is just remember who you are. There is no point in looking at whatever is out there and trying to compare yourself. You want to bring something new to the table, so just stay focused on your own path. That's the main thing.

Growing up, how did your faith help you overcome struggles of confidence or the fear of failure? Again, my mum taught me to find faith in God to overcome my fears. I have loved singing from a young age but I wasn't confident in sharing it. My mum would just say, 'Look, what are you afraid of? You know you have God behind you. You have Jesus with you. What are you afraid of? Just go out there and show people what you can do. God has blessed you with this gift.' Any time I've been scared, I always prayed and asked God to guide me. I always find that the path is always made clearer. So I just have faith and I know that he's always guiding me in the right direction.

You grew up with an English father and a Ghanaian mother. Was there any fears or battles faced internally or externally due to these two sides of your heritage? Yeah. That was interesting, actually, because there weren't many people growing up that were from, like, a dual-heritage background. I had white friends, black friends, Asian friends – there weren't many people in the middle. I was sometimes asked which side of my heritage I identify with. What kind of question is that? I would say, 'I'm mixed-race. My mum's black. My dad's white.' I don't really say I'm one or the other. Why can't I just be who I am? I'm fortunate to be raised by both my parents and they both taught me about both cultures. But I guess that was something that I faced growing up.

Fear of failure can often lead to fear of risk-taking. I know you've mentioned The X Factor, but would you say you've taken any risks more recently? This year has been a big one for risk-taking for me. I have recently left Syco Records, my record label. I felt that creatively me and the team at the label were all going in different directions, but it was a risk because it can feel comforting to have a big-name label behind you. I got to a point where I was like, 'Music is my first love and I need to get my music out there.' I took a risk in taking control and bringing up that conversation with the label. Ultimately, it was a very amicable split and we both agreed that it was the best thing to do. But I think that a lot of people in the industry are too scared to do that because you're scared to not have a label. You're scared to have that tag of being 'dropped'. But I know not to be defined by that. Now I feel like a boss

being 'dropped'. But I know not to be in the situation, because I can decide know that God's just going to lead me home; I'll find where I need to be. **"**

in the situation, because I can decide which direction to take my music in. I know that God's just going to lead me on the right path and I'll find my home; I'll find where I need to be.

How do you feel you've dealt with the pressures of expectation placed on you by others because of the success you've had? Insane. I felt like the pressure of being on *The X Factor* was enough. But then as soon as I came off the show I realized that I was in the real world and everyone expected me to then be a massive superstar – overnight! I felt a lot of pressure releasing my first single because I had already had a number 1 on iTunes, covering someone else's song, which was amazing. But then it was like, 'Oh my gosh, now you need to go and do your own music.' I remember praying through that whole experience and just sort of saying, 'Look, God, if this is what I'm supposed to do, then let your will be done.' That has been a comfort that's helped me overcome expectations.

What do you feel God is calling you to use music for? I need to let people know that you can be a Christian and you can be

in the industry as long as you're strong in your faith. There is no reason why you can't be there. I think a lot of young Christians are told it's a dark industry and question whether they can really pursue a life in entertainment and still have a strong faith. I guess I am one of those examples that show, yes, you can.

Can you remember a specific season where you felt the fear of failure? I remember when I left university in order to pursue my singing, I got a job in a nightclub where I waitressed for about two years. Throughout that time people would look at me with pity, telling me that I should be doing something more with my life. I constantly had to defend myself to live up to other people's expectations.

No one really bought it when I said I really wanted to sing. There was also loads of temptation with alcohol and crazily late nights and I remember my mum really wanting me to quit.

I remember constantly praying for God to show me if it was the right thing and one day, when I went to see a vocal coach and my voice was shattered, the coach asked me, 'Do you really want to pursue music?' I said yes, and she said, 'Is your voice always like that after a shift at the club?' I nodded, and she said, 'Hate to break it to you, but if you want to be a singer, you're going to have to stop working there.' I was like woah! There's a clear sign from God.

Literally that same week, I got a phone call to do DJ Fresh's Live Lounge on BBC Radio 1, and after that he asked me to be part of his live band. God is so good!

And obviously you must have faced the fear of failure in *The X Factor*? Of course, and I didn't have any faith support in the house. No one really spoke about faith there. One of the vocal coaches, Camille Purcell, was a Christian. When she saw me at *X Factor* for the second time, she was so happy to see me, and she always encouraged me, saying things like, 'Fleur, keep the faith. You know God's got amazing things coming for you.'

In terms of the judges' and the public's rejection, I kind of just went onto autopilot. Something just switched in me and I was kind of like a machine. I was *so* focused, everything would just bounce off me. Nothing really affected me that badly.

Do you think people inside the industry have noticed a difference in you because of your faith? Yeah. It's interesting, actually. Even when I left the label I got a message from a colleague there that said, 'I've never met anyone like you. In this industry, you spread light and positivity wherever you go. There's something really special about you.' My vocal coach Joshua is also a Christian and says that some people in the industry have commented about the positivity that follows me, which I think all stems from my faith.

What would you say to young people fearing failure, through whatever industry or situation, to help them overcome it? I think God blesses all of us with gifts, regardless of what they are, and if you've got a gift you shouldn't let fear stop you from stepping into that. I know people who did and they have regrets that they didn't live the life they thought was marked out for them. Have faith that God only wants to guide you in a direction that is good for you and he will be with you every step of the way. Don't deny yourself the right to follow what your calling is. Don't let fear dictate your part. Don't give fear that sort of power.

> **Don't deny yourself the right to follow what your calling is. Don't let fear dictate your part. Don't give fear that sort of power.**

FEAR NOT,
FOR I AM
WITH YOU;
BE NOT
DISMAYED,
FOR I AM
YOUR GOD;
I WILL
STRENGTHEN
YOU, I WILL
HELP YOU, I
WILL UPHOLD
YOU WITH MY
RIGHTEOUS
RIGHT HAND.

ISAIAH 41:10 (ESV)

G
U
V
N
A

"I think the biggest fears are around identity.
I feel like the youth are scared of being
who God created them to be."

FEAR OF FAILURE

> ❝I was definitely scared of not fitting in, being an outcast or being different. I always felt like I was a bit different and had that insecurity.❞

What's your full name?
Isaac Charles Borquaye

Where were you born?
Custom House in east London, E16. We didn't have much, but it was like a little family. I grew up on an estate so everyone knew everyone – a lot of the people there were first-generation Brits with their parents moving over from places like Ghana, Nigeria and Jamaica.

What do you do? I'm predominantly a rapper. But everything I do is geared towards helping young people reach their full potential whether through music, youth work or online.

What are your hobbies?
Outside of the stuff I do for work... I quite like Hoovering; I find it therapeutic! I like watching football. Standard stuff to be honest. I'm very indoorsy – I've never camped in my life! Maybe it's 'cause I travel so much ...when I'm home, I just prefer to be home.

Who inspires you to be fearless and why? Anyone that goes against the grain and fights for what is right – Martin Luther King, Jesus – obviously. Musically, Kirk Franklin because he's uncompromising and authentic. Jerry Lorenzo as well; he runs a fashion company called Fear of God. They're a mainstream brand but unapologetically Christian. My wife, Emma, inspires me as well. She runs an organization called Girl Got Faith that aims to give young girls the confidence to dream big and escape the pressures, expectations or stereotypes that society may place on them.

Were you scared of anything as a child? I was definitely scared of not fitting in, being an outcast or being different. I always felt like I was a bit different and had that insecurity. It started with silly things. I remember sitting in my bed and being really upset that my real name was Isaac because no one at my school was called Isaac. And then it was because my parents were from Ghana, then because I had a gap in my teeth. I was definitely scared of not fitting in.

What's the biggest risk you've taken? Probably going into the career I'm in and just being me. All my peers were talking about the usual stuff, like money, girls and drugs, and so it felt like a risk to rap about what I stand for.

Do you have any key verses in the Bible that help you overcome fear? My favourite verses always change. At the moment, Colossians 3:23. It says, 'Anything you do, work at it wholeheartedly, as if you're doing it for God, and not for human masters.' Sometimes we do things because of fear of failure or rejection but doing things for God's glory frees us from that. Also, James 4:7, which says, 'If you resist the devil, he will flee from you and if you draw close to God, he'll draw close to you.'

Have you received any advice about overcoming fear? if so, what was it? Sometimes the best advice isn't that groundbreaking, but is just gentle reminders like, 'Focus on God,' and 'You can do anything through God who gives you the strength to do it.'

What do you think is powerful and important about remembering the greatness and goodness of God? When you know who God is, it's life-changing. He's like a solid rock, something that never changes. Seasons will change but God is always the same. And when you've got something that solid in your life, you can remind yourself of it when times are tough.

What do you see as the biggest fear the youth are facing today? I think the biggest fears are around identity. I feel like the youth are scared of being who God created them to be. Even if they're not scared, they're confused because we live in a time where you feel like you can't say, 'This is what I believe', without offending someone. There's so much noise of the 'general consensus' on our timelines that I feel like young people struggle to think for themselves and find out who God really wants them to be. Jesus had divisive opinions but because of his confidence, wisdom and authenticity, lots of people listened to him.

How do you hope your work will impact that and encourage people? For many youth it can feel like there's two sides in life: popular culture and things like faith that tend to go against the flow – unpopular culture. A lot of the time youth can be bombarded with popular culture which makes it hard to stand up for what you believe. So I try my hardest to encourage young people by putting out positive messages. Because I know that the majority of the time the more positivity you hear, the more godly content you hear, the more you're likely to be drawn to it.

I go into schools for people of all faiths and none and do sessions on music, peer pressure, staying safe online, identity, maintaining your integrity and authenticity. A lot of the values in the Bible aren't exclusive to Christians so I don't want the encouragements to be exclusive.

What do you think about hope in today's culture that tells us to put hope in things like our relationship status, career success and the likes? Hope is light at the end of the tunnel. Hope is saying that you don't have to live your life the way that culture tells us to, but there is actually another way. To someone that's in a dark place, to someone that's had broken relationships or comes from a broken home, that hope is going to be everything.

How have you experienced the fear of failure in your career? Primarily, the initial fear I experienced in my career was the fear of failing my parents. They're both Ghanaian and worked their socks off to come over here to give me and my younger brother the best opportunities possible. Then one day I come home and say I'm going to be a rapper! I kind of tried to please my parents by going through the traditional university route, studying business management and journalism, and did my music stuff on the side. Now I look back and think if I was a bit bolder then I might be a bit further along than I am now musically. But, on the other hand, I still believe that trying to please my parents and obey them had its benefits.

> **There's definitely a fear there because I know I have a platform and don't want to make a mistake that would turn people away from faith. I just try my best to push into God and say, 'Help me to live with integrity.' Nobody's perfect.**

Did you feel any fear of failure when you first started to rap about your faith? Yeah. The weird thing is I felt fear of failure and rejection from both sides. At school I was being encouraged to rap about the stuff that everyone else raps about like street violence or girls. And at church I was being encouraged to make every single song about Jesus. And in reality I didn't want to do either. So what happened is I compromised on both sides. So I just had to be brave and just be true to myself. I want to make music that gives people hope and inspires people to want to be better versions of themselves. Some of that overtly mentions Jesus; some of it is just about the values he preached. At the end of the day, I'm going to do what I feel God wants me to do. Sometimes the church places just as much pressure on us as society does. And so we've just got to make sure that we're not being influenced by religion or popular culture, but we're being influenced by the Bible, Jesus and the people that really know us and care about us and that we're accountable to.

Did you fear failure when publishing your first book *Unpopular Culture*? One hundred percent! With music, you get to hide behind the beat and the microphone, but without it it's just you. Also, I hate writing – I had the choice in uni to do a dissertation or take an extra module, and I did the extra work! I had a fear that people would think it was rubbish, but I felt like I had an important message and I wanted to put it out there.

What advice would you give the next generation wanting to follow a God given dream but feeling fearful? If you could give them a personal message, what would you say? Even though I'm on stage a lot, I'm a really shy person. When I first thought about doing music I was really scared about performing, but I thought to myself, 'Right now I'm not performing. If I do it and it doesn't go well, I'm in the same position – so I may as well try!' My advice would just be: you lose nothing from trying, so just try.

Another piece of advice would be to not try to be like anyone else. Just do what comes naturally to you and what pleases God. There's already a Guvna B, there's already a Rich Wilkerson – so don't try and be anyone else. Be you.

Do you feel the pressure of being a role model? Definitely. There's definitely a fear there because I know I have a platform and I don't want to make a mistake that would turn people away from faith. I just try my best to push into God and just say, 'Help me to live with integrity.' Nobody's perfect.

How did you come to follow Jesus? I was in a chicken shop in east London, and I was about to order my two piece chicken, chips and drink, and then I saw this weird glowing thing in the corner, and it looked like an angel …I'm joking! Some people have really amazing stories but mine is probably more standard for a lot of people. I was raised in a Christian family and messed about for a bit, and then one time the speaker at church asked whether anyone was lukewarm. I was like, 'Oh yeah, that's me.' Then he asked, 'Does anyone want to make a commitment to actually follow Jesus wholeheartedly?' And I was like, 'Yeah, I'll have a go.' And then it went from there. I've had times of feeling like I've got loads of faith and others where I feel low on faith, but every day I want more God. I want to be closer to him.

GROUP DISCUSSION ✗ QUESTIONS
CHAPTER 1 FEAR OF FAILURE

'See me.' When Jo read those two words splashed in red across her university paper, she was immediately filled with dread. Without even knowing the context of those words, Jo was already questioning her ability to continue the course. She was already fearing failure.

Let's be real: nobody enjoys failing. Nobody enjoys setting their eyes on a goal, working hard and falling short. Nobody enjoys their shortcoming being displayed for the world to see. Yet a degree of failure is an intrinsic part of the human experience. Being fallible creatures means that we won't act perfectly in our every endeavour (and it's not only that we won't, it's that we can't). The fear of failure (often known as atychi-phobia), however, is a deep-set insecurity that creates overpowering self-doubt and shuts us down – and in some cases even causes us to subconsciously sabotage our own chances for success. The desire to move away from a negative consequence of trying overshadows the desire to move towards the positive outcome.

The fear of failure is tightly connected with ridicule, rejection and loneliness, and it has plagued us from the dawn of time. When the first humans fell from their place of perfection before God (Genesis 3), they immediately knew they had failed him. Fearing ridicule, they covered themselves; fearing rejection, they hid. Their failure brought on a fear of ridicule and rejection, but their effort to escape looming loneliness only

drove them to become lonelier still.

We must remember, however, that failure doesn't make us somehow less human. On the contrary, it can be harnessed to make us more human. Not only does failure, when properly utilized, help guide us towards what is required for success (we are reminded of Thomas Edison's consideration of his perceived failure to get successful results: 'I have gotten a lot of results. I know several thousand things that won't work!'), but it can also be used to build our internal qualities like perseverance, creativity and even compassion. Use failure well, and it can become a better strength than success.

REFLECTION QUESTIONS

1. Why do we fear failure?
2. How can the fear of failure negatively affect our lives and the lives of those around us?
3. Read Romans 5:3. How does Paul view failure ('sufferings')? How does he see failure as a stepping stone to success?
4. Peter was a profound failure. Though boldly declaring his unwavering support of Jesus (Matthew 26), he quickly succumbed to fear and denied him, failing Jesus in his time of need (Luke 22). But read John 21. How does Jesus respond to Peter's failure? How does this help quell our fear of failing before God?
5. Each of us needs champions who help us lift our heads after a failure and encourage us to try again. Who are three people who are your champions? What made you think of them as your champions?*
6. Just as others are champions to us and help us rebound after a failure, we are also meant to be champions to others. Who are three people (it could be more!) that you are committed to championing, regardless of their failures?*

* Seek out those three people that you named as champions to you and thank them for what they have done and how they have spoken louder than the voice of failure. Seek out those people you are committed to championing and tell them in no uncertain terms that you are committed to making sure they know their past, present and future failures will never affect your love for them. Tell them that as long as you live, failure will not be the loudest voice they hear!

CHAPTER 2 FEAR OF RIDICULE

"BE STRONG AND COURAGEOUS. DO NOT FEAR OR BE IN DREAD OF THEM, FOR IT IS THE LORD YOUR GOD WHO GOES WITH YOU. HE WILL NOT LEAVE YOU OR FORSAKE YOU." DEUTERONOMY 31:6 (ESV)

CHAPTER 2

FEAR OF
RIDICULE

BY: PHIL KYEI

Your mum is...

Your face looks like...

You look like a...

We've all had the experience

of being laughed at by our

friends, people we work

with, members of our own

family. Occasionally, you

may even recall being

laughed at by a stranger.

Being laughed at by others can be a miserable experience. Call it bullying, teasing or mocking out, serving as the butt of someone else's humour is tough on the human soul. What's worse, this kind of mistreatment by others can lead people to become anxious and fearful of being exposed to the situation again. At the same time, you start to wonder whether there's something wrong with you and so start to question your own personal qualities.

Allowing ridicule to take hold of your life stops you from being the person you were designed to be. We either fear the ridicule we know will come, or we get discouraged when the name-calling comes. Instead of persevering and pushing through we hold back, retreat and surrender.

There have been many times in my life where I hesitated or in some cases completely pulled back from opportunities to share my faith because I was afraid of being made fun of or having my faith insulted. We cry out to God in moments like these for him to change our circumstances. But God is far more interested in changing your mind than changing your circumstances.

We always want God to change our circumstances; we want him to take away our problems, all our sufferings and the things we are going through. And God says, 'Yes, but what is really more important is what happens to you. I am far more interested in changing your mind before I change your circumstances.' Because nothing ever happens in life until you get a renewed mind.

No transformation in your life can ever take place until your thoughts begin to change. When we understand that the power of God's word is way more potent than the word of man we can begin to be free of the fear of ridicule.

The Bible says the power of the mind, the power of your thoughts, has a tremendous ability to shape your life for good or for bad. If you accept ridicule or took to heart things that were said over you when you were younger – that you were worthless, that you'd never amount

to much – whether it is true or not, those thoughts will remain captive in your mind. And what begins to happen is that we live life governed by these thoughts in our head. Letting God manage our minds is actually the key to peace and the key to happiness. An unmanaged mind leads to tension; a managed mind leads to tranquillity. The unmanaged mind leads to pressure, but the managed mind leads to peace. An unmanaged mind leads to conflict and chaos, but a managed mind leads to strength, to security and to serenity.

So what do I do if I want to have a healthy mind, when I want to have my mind renewed? Ultimately you must feed your mind with the truth. We all know the importance of nutrition. Good food and calories cause you to be better, look better, to be stronger and to be healthier, for you to have more energy. Bad choices, on the other hand, can harm our bodies. The same is true for our thought lives. I must feed my mind not with junk and poison but with the truth. And what does the Bible say about truth: 'The truth will set you free' (John 8:31–32).

When do you take this antidote to the bad thoughts in your life? Do you take it once a week when you come to church? When you are feeling bad? The answer is all the time. Throughout the day, the morning and the night.

It is our choice and our decision to think in the way we should think. You have to believe that God's word is for you. And you need to hear yourself saying what you actually believe. Words have power. That's why ridicule packs such a punch, but God's word and God's truth over you is stronger. It takes time, perseverance and endurance and these are things the Bible talks about. Don't quit after one day of failure. Instead get back up again and continue to endeavour, continue to seek the things of God. I want to choose to speak life into my life. I want to know that in Christ there is always a hope. I want to see myself as a victor, as an overcomer. You make that daily decision to speak life into your life instead of the words of doubts.

PHIL KYEI is the Location Pastor of Hillsong's New Bermondsey campus. A Londoner through and through, Phil left the banking sector seven years ago to serve the church full time. Though he has served in multiple roles throughout these years, Phil has always been about building the local church and communicating the word of God in a relevant understandable way.

DO NOT SAY, "I AM ONLY A YOUTH"; FOR TO ALL TO WHOM I SEND YOU, YOU SHALL GO, AND WHATEVER I COMMAND YOU, YOU SHALL SPEAK. DO NOT BE AFRAID OF THEM, FOR I AM WITH YOU TO DELIVER YOU, DECLARES THE LORD.

JEREMIAH 1:7-8 (ESV)

MARIAISABEL
RODRIGUEZ
POSITIVELY SHAPING SOCIETY X L.A.

HILLSONG YOUTH X YOUNG ADULTS

FEAR OF RIDICULE

"IF I GOT THROUGH THIS WITH MY EYES FOCUSED ON GOD, IMAGINE ALL THE OTHER STUFF I WILL BE ABLE TO OVERCOME."

Where were you born?
Indio, California, USA

What do you do?
I am a high school student, currently in my junior year, and an intern for a fashion company called Father Daughter LA.

What hobbies do you have?
I started my own magazine, *The Sparrow*, with my best friend. I love writing and reading, designing and anything in the creative field.

Who inspires you to be fearless and why?
Carmen Yulin Cruz Soto inspires me to be fearless. She is currently the Mayor of San Juan, Puerto Rico, and I admire her as a woman and politician. Being a woman of colour, she faces a lot of backlash for being in a high-powered position and for standing up for what is right. During Hurricane Maria, which devastated Puerto Rico in 2017, Carmen fearlessly walked through deep waters to help her people.

What were you scared of as a child? I was scared of the future. I grew up with just my mom and brother because my parents divorced when I was little. I feared what my future would look like without my father in it.

What's the biggest risk you've taken? Telling my mom that I wanted to keep going back to Hillsong and that I wanted to get baptized as a Christian there. In their eyes, that meant that I was abandoning my family and betraying the Catholic Church. Throughout this time I also risked losing friends and facing the backlash from my wider family. Though it was tough, I learned to separate what was godly from what was not. I focused my energy and time into people who helped me, encouraged me and guided me in my walk with Christ, and I distanced myself from those who did not help me grow in my faith.

Do you have a Key verse you live by to overcome fear?
'Don't let the excitement of youth cause you to forget your Creator.' Ecclesiastes 12:1. I think as youth it is important not to get too caught up in the earthly things around us. With all the worldly opportunities and distractions around us, we are often tempted to steer our eyes from him and fall off our God-given path. I love this verse as it reminds us to not fear missing out on the earthly things that will threaten living an eternity with him.

Have you received advice about overcoming fear?
One of my leaders, Alexandra, once told me that whatever hardships I overcome will become part of my testimony that in the future will help others overcome theirs. I will be able to look back and say, 'If I got through this with my eyes focused on God, imagine all the other stuff I will be able to overcome.'

Do you have a favourite book that's helped you on your spiritual journey?
Uninvited by Lysa TerKeurst in which she encourages us that by keeping our eyes focussed on God we can overcome more than we can imagine.

There seems to be a culture of ridicule everywhere. You just need to look at the news. How do you think it can breed division and hatred among people of differing opinion? I think our current political divisions in the US are a great example of how the actions of people in power can affect the views of others. The sad truth is that we let this ridicule between different sides increase the divide in our views instead of bringing us together in unity and love. I love this quote by A.W. Tozer: 'We cannot pray in love and live in hate and still think we are worshipping God.' I think it is an important reminder for Christ followers – it is okay to have different opinions but it should not cause division.

From your perspective, can you help people understand what it's like for US Mexicans living in America today? As much as I love my motherland, we can't forget that America was founded on innocent blood and oppression. Minorities have been ridiculed and belittled for decades. This has become such a norm, and some have even become accustomed to the lies. Some of the stereotypes that are usually placed on Hispanics are that they are all lazy, they are drug dealers, they are not smart etc. Hearing this over and over can cause you to believe it, but I choose not to. I won't let people label me. I won't let them put me in a box because I choose to rise above it.

What do you think about the culture that tells us to do whatever you can to be accepted and praised or you'll be ridiculed and rejected? Our society has been conditioned to change the way we are or the way we look in order to fit in with the rest. God did not create us to assimilate. He created us to stand out. He made us the way we are for a reason. Surround yourself with Christ-minded people who will uplift you in the good and bad and who will love you for you.

How has your relationship with Jesus redefined how you view ridicule and the fear of it? I am confident in who I am because I know I am made in his image. There are days

when the words hurt but I remember that the hurt is temporary and God's word is eternal.

Thinking back over your life, what have been the biggest things that have come against you in terms of being ridiculed? I was born in the United States and I come from a Hispanic family. I have battled with having these two identities over and over and have often been told hurtful things about my heritage.

During the presidential elections and even to this day, the comments that were being made about Latinos really hit home. I felt ashamed even though I knew these views were not true. Before I was rooted in Christ, I never

"YOU KNOW YOUR WORTH. YOU KNOW THAT YOU ARE LOVED NO MATTER WHAT. THAT YOU ARE FORGIVEN AHEAD OF TIME. THAT YOU WERE MADE BY HIM IN HIS IMAGE BEFORE YOU WERE EVEN BORN. KNOWING ALL THIS, THERE IS NOTHING THAT YOU CANNOT OVERCOME. IT IS CRAZY TO THINK THAT HIS LOVE IS INFINITE AND UNCONDITIONAL – WE DON'T DESERVE IT! "

liked to say that I was Hispanic, but at the same time due to my fair skin I was sometimes told I was not Mexican enough. Through Christ, I learnt to accept all sides of myself and background as it makes me who he intended me to be. When I am with my church family I feel loved and accepted as I am.

Have you faced ridicule at school for your faith?
I am very open about my faith at school. Sometimes I get mocked for it but I choose not to listen. Even though some people hate it when I talk about God, there are others that know they can come to me with questions or prayer requests. Even if it is just one peer, I am helping bring revival in the city of L.A.

What is the power of defining yourself as a child of God, where he doesn't judge or ridicule but loves you unconditionally?
You know your worth. You know that you are loved no matter what. That you are forgiven ahead of time. That you were made by him in his image before you were even born. Knowing all this, there is nothing that you cannot overcome. It is crazy to think that his love is infinite and unconditional – we don't deserve it! But yet his grace constantly reminds us that he died for us, so therefore we deserve it and we need to fulfil our God-given paths.

Tell us about prayer in connecting with God, especially in times that can be fearful? When times get hard and I am fearful, I turn my eyes to God and I completely surrender. It is so easy to question him, asking, 'Why God?' or 'Why are you doing this?' instead of saying, 'Lord give me the strength to get through this.' Prayers are so powerful. It is my one-on-one with God in which I can tell him all my problems that he has already worked out. Instead of asking the whys, I pray for him to put love, forgiveness and understanding in my heart so I can overcome the season and come out stronger.

By praying, I was able to forgive the people who have hurt me; I was able to know my worth and be confident in my identity, and I was able to flourish as a woman of God.

This God –
his way is perfect;
the word of the Lord
proves true; he is a

SHIELD

for all those who
take refuge in him.

PSALM 18:30 (ESV)

MARCEL

"My mum never said, 'You can't. You shouldn't. You're not good at it.' She never had that mentality. I always believed that anything was possible."

FEAR OF RIDICULE

Where are you from?
I was born in Senegal, lived there, moved around for a bit and came to Paris when I was about fourteen. I stayed there until I was eighteen, then I came to London.

And how old are you now? I'm 29. How time flies!

Where did you study fashion? I never studied fashion. My mum had factories when I was young and she is a super-fashionable, elegant lady. I probably didn't realize it was my calling until about five years ago. Even though I'd always liked fashion, I didn't realize it was what God was asking me to do. It just kind of happened.

Do you classify yourself as a creative director or a designer? I personally don't like titles. I wouldn't say I'm a 'designer' because everything I do is a collaboration with different people, so I'm just a young creative. I just put ideas together and get people to grasp my vision to put it on paper.

What's your relationship with God like? I've had a really strong relationship with God from a young age. I always believed, even if I didn't go to church. I always prayed. I prayed for people. I prayed for everybody. I feel like a child of God. Everyone has to feel special in their own way. My relationship was so strong that I've never been afraid of anything. I've been part of four-car accidents, I've been in a country in war and I've overcome all of that. I was born in a small village in Africa. What my mum overcame to even allow me to be here – it's like winning the lottery. So therefore when you've been through all those journeys and you're where you are, everything that happens to you is small. It's irrelevant. And that's my story. And I'm not afraid of anything. I'm like, if I'm able to be here today, I can overcome any situation.

What were you scared of as a child? After I grew up I realized that you shouldn't be afraid of things, but as a child I was always afraid of failure. I was also afraid of losing my mum. I remember she used to travel a lot and every time she did I was afraid she would never come back. I used to have sleepless nights – just afraid. When she came back it was a relief.

> **My relationship was so strong that I've never been afraid of anything. I've been part of four-car accidents, I've been in a country in war and I've overcome all of that.**

What do you feel has been the biggest risk you've taken? My fashion label, because before I started it I had a really good job. I was about 24, 25, and I was earning good money. I was comfortable. I literally took all my money and just said, 'You know what? I'm going to leave this job and I'm going to start a fashion label.' At which point I understood nothing about fashion. In my heart I knew I couldn't lead my life working for somebody. I always said, 'If you don't follow your dream and work for your dream, somebody else will hire you to follow theirs.' I wanted to be able to do my own thing. So I took all my savings and put them into my brand.

Have you received any advice on overcoming fear? I was always so protected when I was with my mum that I never grew up with that feeling of fear. I don't know how to explain it. I wanted to play football, my mum was like, 'Play football.' I wanted to do something else, she'd encourage me to do it. My mum never said, 'You can't. You shouldn't. You're not good at it.' She never had that mentality. I always believed that anything was possible.

So those parameters weren't put on you? Yeah. I never had any. It was only

when I got here [to London], that's when I felt like, 'Okay, everything that she was telling me before is now reality, so I have to grow up.' I didn't speak a word of English. I spent all my money. I did everything – washing plates, counting the pennies to buy pasta right to the point where I thought, 'I'm going to go back to Paris.' Then I thought, 'Well, I can't, because if I go, this is failing and for my mum it's going to be like, this is your son. He went, failed and came back.' And then God came through. By accident, I found a job collecting glasses. But like I said, when I collected a glass I wanted to be the best at it. When I was best at it they made me a barman. And when I was best at that they made me a waiter. And when I was best at that I was a nightclub floor manager, then became a general manager. During the whole process of it, I was trying to be excellent at everything I was doing. That all came from my mum's mentality.

Can you relate to fear of rejection? As a human being, you always want to be accepted. You're not made to live alone so everything we do is to be accepted and recognized. So when you wear your nice pair of shoes, it's not for yourself, it's just for society to accept you. So I guess in everyday life, we're actually

living in fear of rejection. We're afraid of being rejected by society. That fear is around us constantly. I've felt it, I can't lie to you. There's a few things you do. Most of the time, when you wake up in the morning, the first thing you do is you pick up your phone. It's the last thing we do at night, and that fills our subconscious.

As a creative, is it hard balancing your unshakable value as a child of God with the fact that people can choose whether or not they like your work, which feels very personal? When I started out, it was hard. After going through things, I've just learned to accept it. Now it's like, I'm not making stuff to please you. I'm making stuff so you accept my art as it is. But at first it was; it was like a big battle of acceptance. And sometimes because I'm super-competitive, I make stuff and then I might see a brand that's doing great, better than me, and I'm thinking, 'What I'm doing is twenty times better than this.' It's a constant battle, but I've learned. I'm trying and still learning.

What have you felt has really helped you get moving in terms of learning that? God really opening my mind. I'm hungry to really open my mindset. To be honest, what I listen to every day be-

fore I go to bed, when I wake up and direct my focus towards God – all that helps me witness God, see God, at work more. Everything happens because God is there and he makes it happen. On my clothes you can see there are a lot of Bible verses and quotes, but people probably don't realize.

With regard to the label, Marr London, tell me about the slogan: 'Marr Don't Care'? I think that slogan was produced during a tipping point where I started really finding myself and came to a place of thinking, 'I'm going to do what I like.' You like it, you don't, it's okay. I understand. You've got to have an opinion. Either negative or positive. It's fine. If you don't have an opinion, I'm not happy. That's when we thought, we're going to do whatever we want. If you have an opinion or not, it's okay – I don't care.

Tell me a bit more about the messages on the clothes. You mentioned about using scriptures in your work. Did that begin when you came back to church? I love it when I'm in church. Sometimes when I go there the preacher says stuff

and I get inspired. One message I stand for – which I think is the whole message to young people – is: 'Be yourself.' The Bible says it a lot. It gives you advice to be yourself following God, be yourself, be free. I refuse to be put in a box, where society decides girls should wear skirts. If you look back in history, men started wearing heels before girls because rich men wanted to look tall. So I refuse to be in that box. I'm going to live my life how I want to, but obviously with morals. I want to be good to others and help where I can as much as I can. And sharing, caring about people, about humanity. That's what my clothes reflect, really. The art, the scriptures, everything it says . . . the message is all about that.

Is that part of the dream for the fashion label long term: how you can communicate that message? It's almost like you're a preacher but you're doing it through clothes. It's about creating clothing that will spark opinions, open up the conversation. My biggest dream is probably to open orphanages, where those kids get to be themselves and not have structured school education. I feel like going to school is like taking a monkey, a lion and a crocodile and saying, 'Okay, you climb a tree. Whoever climbs it best, this is the result,' instead of finding out what you're good at as an individual and pushing you in that direction to use the best of your ability.

Do you find designing and art a way of overcoming fear by being completely free in what you create? Definitely. Because while I'm doing it, it allows me to just be. Probably a few years back I wouldn't have been able to speak to you the way I'm speaking now. Doing this has opened a lot of doors for me. It made me feel comfortable in myself even though I used to be shy if I didn't know people. I remember when I was younger I used to go into a shop, buy

something, and the person was there, and I wasn't afraid of them. I was just in my zone because I was always a dreamer. I always felt like I was a stranger – awkward.

What advice would you give the next generation wanting to follow a dream but feeling fearful? Don't let anybody kill that dream. The word 'can't' shouldn't exist. Just 'do'. Just have a dream. Have something worth waking up for every morning. It doesn't matter what you do. Don't let anybody tell you can't. Just believe and be fearless, and put God first. Don't let society believe that you're worthless. Be fearless and just do.

Can you share a time where God has helped you through a difficult time? The most recent one was a moment where I was sitting on my sofa, so depressed, and just wanting to give up. And literally I saw this light of Jesus just holding my hand and saying, 'Listen, it's going to work.' And every single day, I promise you, when I ask myself, 'How am I going to do this because it's so hard to pay for this?' – orders come up. Stuff that never happens.

What would you say to someone who loves God but doesn't have a dad in their life and has some bad influences there instead? I would say to them that you've got to keep believing. You're not master of your circumstance, but you're master of your mind. Your father's not here, but maybe the father not being here is the reason you are who you are. Don't be angry. Don't be afraid. Don't listen to these people. You've got to get out and dream big. And know what your purpose is in life. You can't be a human being with no purpose. But nobody's perfect, right? People make mistakes. Things are going to happen but you learn from it. And just keep going.

God met me

more than halfway,

he freed me

from my anxious fears.

Look at him;

give him your warmest smile.

Never hide

your feelings from him.

When I was desperate,

I called out,

and God got me out of

a tight spot.

God's angel sets up

a circle of protection

around us while we pray.

PSALM 34:4-7 (MSG)

I CALLED OUT, AND

GOD GOT ME OUT

LEAH
McFALL

"As a younger generation, we need to absolutely know the word of God, so we're well equipped to deal with these lies and these fears that are spoken over us."

FEAR OF RIDICULE

What's your full name?
Leah McFall

Where were you born?
Northern Ireland

What do you do?
I'm a singer-songwriter – which kind of makes it sound like I play an instrument and I don't!

What are your hobbies?
I really love knitting! I think it's because it combines my other hobby of sitting and binge-watching series – it's basically an excuse for getting to do that. I knit hats and mittens for my husband who has to wear them because he loves me.

Who inspires you to be fearless and why? A good few people, but I'd say mostly my mum because we've been through a lot together. We've had a lot of loss and heartache in our family but her faith is so steadfast. She started studying social work at the age of thirty. Some people would tell themselves they were too old to start something new like that, but she graduated top of her class and has been promoted so many times. She also hates public speaking but because of her testimony she's been asked to speak at churches and stuff, and she just says yes to whatever God asks her to do!

Were you scared of anything as a child? I was actually less afraid of performing than I am now. So I probably had childhood fears of things like heights and stuff, but as I got older the fears become more about yourself and what you can and can't do.

What's the biggest risk you've taken? Probably going on The Voice. I'd been singing for years, but I was really worried about going on a 'talent show' because I thought that it might discredit my artistic side. I'd also been told by the record company that owned the show that my voice was like Marmite. People were either going to love it or hate it. I felt like I was preparing to find out the answer to that question – in front of nine million people! I was also really nervous about the press attention the show attracts. My family has seen a lot of tragedy in the past and I was worried that they would bring it all up publicly. I was really frightened. I knew it was going to be in front of a lot of people, and I was just worried about how it would work out.

Whenever I prayed about whether God wanted me to go on the show or not, I never got a definite answer. I just really felt him saying, 'It doesn't matter. Whichever way you go, I'll be with you.' And he was. I got up at 5am every morning of the show to spend time with God. I was literally on my knees, like, 'I just need to have a sentence from you today that I can absolutely hold onto because this is the scariest thing I've ever done.' And there was never a morning where he didn't give me one.

> ## "We've had a lot of loss and heartache in our family but [my mum's] faith is so steadfast."

Can you tell us a bit about the fears you faced during your time on the show? Fear of rejection, failure and ridicule for sure. You've got the media coming up with these headlines of stuff you never said. You're being embarrassed by that, and you come to fear ridicule from the public. At the same time, you're absolutely terrified of being rejected so publicly – and it's not rejecting your career plans, it's rejecting your dream. Then there's failure – the fear that you make a mistake or your voice fails. You want to walk off that stage knowing you've done a good job.

Can you tell us a bit about your journey with fear during the aftermath of the show? Immediately after the show I was sent to L.A. and was writing with some of the top songwriters in the world – it was an incredible experience. In many ways, though, I don't think I was prepared for how political the industry is. I suddenly went from being a singer on a show to being a product that people would fight over. You were told not to take it personally, but it was very, very personal. It was you. I was scared of letting myself and others down, but the other predominant fear was loneliness. I lived in a hotel room by myself for the best part of a year.

Did that experience draw you closer to God or further away? I don't think I fell away from God but I did realize how much you need fellowship. There's a reason God designed the Church and it's actually for our spiritual wellbeing. I prayed hard for somebody in this new environment to be a Christian who I'd be able to talk to about my faith and pray with. The next day this girl showed up and she was a Christian – a brilliant girl who I wrote some of my best songs with. I knew God had poured so much favour on me during the show and so when things got difficult I did question why things weren't going smoothly. My mum just kept on telling me, 'God didn't bring you this far to leave you.'

How did God's word in the Bible help you through this time? Have you got any key verses that spoke to you? One of the things that God had put into me before the show and I never really understood was the verse: 'You're my special possession,' where God is speaking to his people. And at that time I felt like everyone was fighting over who owned me, this verse kept coming into my head: 'You're my special possession, you're my treasure.' In the discussions where I was treated as a product, I held on to the fact that I was God's, that I wasn't owned by anybody but God, who loved me and called me his treasure.

I remember being terrified at the start of The Voice about signing contracts. I remember signing them and thinking, 'God, this can't be right. Surely you don't want me to be bound?' And I just really felt his Spirit say to me, 'There's absolutely no contract that can bind you. There's nothing that can bind you that I can't break when and if I want. So don't be worried. If I want you free, I'll break you free.' And he did. After the show my label dropped me, but me and my music were still signed to my record company. It wasn't easy but eventually God freed me from that contract.

> "But I think it's probably just rejection, isn't it? I think the devil's put that one on us, but he's dressed it up differently with every generation and made new platforms for it to happen. Rejection, failure, ridicule and loneliness are things we all really, really battle. And to be honest with you, you will battle it. You will battle it in whatever industry you're in."

How has God guided you through the unknown throughout your journey? I wish I was one of these people who get visions or has God appear to them in fire. But I feel like all I have heard is a still, quiet voice that I would love to yell at me. And it doesn't. If anything, sometimes I feel like it gets quieter. But that's where you have to quiet yourself. I feel like he sometimes gets quieter so that you quieten down and stop freaking out, because he actually really wants you in a still place.

I've never got an idea of where I'm going to go and everything has been a surprise, and I would love to say that at every single turn I've been like, 'Praise God, I know this is going to be brilliant.' There's been some turns where I've been like, 'God, I think you've made a mistake.' I've questioned every turn. But I don't think he minds that, because I'm always directing my questions at him. I think if I absolutely knew the destination, I think I'd find it hard to do the work to get there. I'd be bored.

Have you received any advice about overcoming fear? Yeah, I definitely have. I've always got really scared about giving a bad performance. And I think Bobby Houston's words have helped me. She says to take a deep breath, breathing out anxiety and breathing in God. Also, to keep remembering who it is all for. Every time I am about to go on stage I always say, 'God, completely for your glory and not for mine.' The stories in the Old Testament also really help. I just love the fact that God always used people that we would never choose for the task.

Would you have any advice for anyone who would want to pursue singing? I went to my pastor before I moved to London to talk about singing and I expected him to be like, 'Nonsense, learn theology and go spread the word of God with your knowledge of scripture,' and all the rest of it. But actually what he said to me was, we need to be looking at the world,

we need to be looking at the industries, and saying, 'Where needs Jesus?' And then we need to go and open our mouths for him once we're in those industries. The music industry absolutely needs more of Jesus. Everybody in every industry needs to know the truth that Jesus loves them and died for them, just to help them to enjoy their lives.

What would you say are the biggest fears that youth are facing today? I think it's literally the same ones that I would have felt. And I know it's a lot more visual because of social media. But I think it's probably just rejection, isn't it? I think the devil's put that one on us, but he's dressed it up differently with every generation and made new platforms for it to happen. Rejection, failure, ridicule and loneliness are things we all really, really battle. And to be honest with you, you will battle it. You will battle it in whatever industry you're in. And it's just about knowing what God has to say on them and having people around you who will tell you when stuff is nonsense.

How did faith change your view of these fears? I remember reading a Joyce Meyer book called *Battlefield of the Mind* and she told the story about the man who was praying whilst demons sat around him whispering lies into his ears. When the man spoke out scripture from his mouth, it came out like swords of light that defeated the darkness and silenced the lies being spoken over him. I just think you have to know your scripture. As a younger generation, we need to absolutely know the word of God, so we're well equipped to deal with these lies and these fears that are spoken over us.

I don't know how many times after walking out from God I've turned back to him and imagined him being so angry. And every single time I've met him, I've been like, 'Oh no, here it comes.' And every time he's just like, 'I love you, I just love you.'

GROUP DISCUSSION ✖ QUESTIONS
CHAPTER 2 FEAR OF RIDICULE

When Leah appeared on *The Voice*, she admits she had a lot to fear – and at the top of her list was the fear of ridicule. Whether we call it teasing, mocking or bullying, being the focal point of someone else's derogatory humour is a miserable experience that few have had the fortune of avoiding. The fear of ridicule (often known as gelotophobia, which literally means the 'fear of laughter') is a deep-seated fear that can cause us to withdraw from social situations – especially highly public situations – where our actions, words and efforts might be derided, lampooned or even scorned. We fear becoming the laughing stock: the one who is ridiculous.

Though a few instances of ridicule might have us questioning our words or actions at the time, ongoing ridicule makes us interrogate our very being. It makes us wonder whether there is something about us as a person that deserves to be mocked. It saps our courage. We question our own worth and value. Over time, we can come to think of ourselves as insignificant, degenerate, irrevocably broken – and not worthy of experiencing true joy and fulfilment, or of bringing such treasure into the lives of others.

The fear of ridicule, while alive to some extent in all of us, is particularly malicious in those who have been, or could be, shamed by someone who they hold in high regard. On the brink of launching her career, Leah was terrified of being embarrassed in front of the public.

Others of us have been shamed by parents or caregivers. Still others have been mocked by employers or others in position of power and influence over us.

It seems that the higher we respect someone, the deeper the betrayal of ridicule penetrates.

Yet God, in his great love for us, has prepared a way for us to overcome the fear of ridicule, and to live free from the power of shame and scorn.

REFLECTION QUESTIONS

1. What effect can ongoing ridicule have in our lives?

2. Why is the ridicule of people we hold in regard particularly painful?

3. God has given us two powerful weapons against ridicule, and the first one might surprise you. Read Romans 12:3. How does Paul instruct us to think about ourselves? What emotion will this guard against? And how might this help us to respond to ridicule?

4. Ridicule wants to cause us great pain and suffering, but that is not God's plan for us. Read Psalm 28:6-7. When David was being mocked, to whom did he turn? What does he mean when he writes that God is his strength and his shield?

5. Each of us needs an encourager, or encouragers, to help us fight the voices of ridicule. Who are three people who are your encouragers? What made you think of them as encouragers?*

6. Just as others are encouragers to us and help us keep ridicule from devouring us, we are also meant to be encouragers to others. Who are three people (it could be more!) you are committed to encouraging, which means to literally 'put courage into' to help them overcome the pains of ridicule?*

* Seek out those people you are committed to encouraging, and tell them in no uncertain terms that you are committed to putting courage into their lives. Tell them that as long as you live, ridicule will not be the loudest voice they hear!

CHAPTER 3 FEAR OF REJECTION

"SO NOW I LIVE WITH THE CONFIDENCE THAT THERE IS NOTHING IN THE UNIVERSE WITH THE POWER TO SEPARATE US FROM GOD'S LOVE. I'M CONVINCED THAT HIS LOVE WILL TRIUMPH OVER DEATH, LIFE'S TROUBLES, FALLEN ANGELS, OR DARK RULERS IN THE HEAVENS. THERE IS NOTHING IN OUR PRESENT OR FUTURE CIRCUMSTANCES THAT CAN WEAKEN HIS LOVE. THERE IS NO POWER ABOVE US OR BENEATH US — NO POWER THAT COULD EVER BE FOUND IN THE UNIVERSE THAT CAN DISTANCE US FROM GOD'S PASSIONATE LOVE, WHICH IS LAVISHED UPON US THROUGH OUR LORD JESUS, THE ANOINTED ONE!" ROMANS 8:38-39 (TPT)

FEAR OF
REJECTION

BY: DAN WATSON
WITH ELIZABETH NEEP

Our society is filled with rejection, so it's no wonder we fear it! Will that girl say yes? Will they still hang out with me? Will anyone 'like' my post? Every day we put ourselves out there and hope that people will like what they see. But how many of us sacrifice our freedom in the face of this fear? How many of us start doing things, going with the flow, just to be accepted, just to be 'liked'? How do we free ourselves from the fear of rejection?

We Need an Antidote

There was a news story recently about a man who was bitten by one of the world's most venomous snakes. One bite contained enough venom to kill a hundred people but fortunately, the man managed to survive. He was treated with an anti-venom within half an hour of the bite. What a great story to tell your mates – though it must have been pretty worrying at the time!

There are all kinds of poisons in the world today, some which our bodies naturally fight and others that require an antidote for the recovery process to begin. But for many of us a poison that affects us greatly is the fear of man – a fear that lies at the very heart of our fear of rejection. The fear of man has the potential to impair and destroy our lives, primarily because it causes us to believe that man has more power over our lives than God. It leads us to believe that whether man accepts or rejects us matters more than whether God does.

Whether it be words spoken over us, actions towards us or gossip behind our back, other people have the potential to cause us all kinds of offence. And we can't stop these voices from coming. The question is, whose voice are you listening to?

The Bible tells us that, 'Fear of man will prove to be a snare, but whoever trusts in the Lord is kept safe' (Proverbs 29:25). We can see then that when it comes to rejection, we have a choice of whether to trust in man or to trust in God. We get to choose who will be the number one voice in our lives, and if we're unsure which one to choose, the Bible tells us what the best choice is: the voice of our creator God!

In life, we can listen and agree with what the crowd says about us, or we can choose to accept what Christ says about us. We can listen to what social media says, or listen to what our Saviour says. We can listen to the words of man, or listen to the word of our Maker. Our heavenly Father says that we are fearfully and wonderfully made; that there is a plan and purpose for our lives; and that greater is he who is in us than he who is in the world.

The best antidote to the fear of man and the fear of rejection by man is the fear of God. Whatever labels people try to put on you, the fear of God shows that you are a child of God, and as soon as you realize that your identity is in Christ, you'll never fall into the trap of listening to the words of man. So what does the Bible tell us about God's view of rejection?

"We can listen
to the words of man,
or **LISTEN** to the Word
of our **MAKER**.
Our heavenly Father says
that we are **FEARFULLY**
and **WONDERFULLY** made;
that there is a plan
and purpose for **OUR LIVES**;
and that greater is
He who is in us
than he who is in
the world."

"WHENEVER YOU FACE REJECTION IT IS GOOD TO REMEMBER THAT JESUS KNOWS EXACTLY HOW YOU FEEL. IN THE GOSPEL OF JOHN IT EVEN SAYS, 'IF THE WORLD HATES YOU, KNOW THAT IT HAS HATED ME BEFORE IT HATED YOU.' IN JESUS, GOD HAS BEEN THERE AND DONE THAT. GOD UNDERSTANDS HOW MUCH IT HURTS TO BE REJECTED. HE UNDERSTANDS BECAUSE HE'S BEEN THERE TOO."

God Knows How You Feel

We know that God is bigger and more powerful than we can imagine, so it can be easy to think that he doesn't understand what it's like to be rejected. But when God sent his Son Jesus to come live on earth, he became a man. Jesus was fully God and yet fully human, meaning he experienced every human emotion we battle with: he got hungry, he got tired, he got teary and he definitely, definitely experienced rejection.

Even before Jesus came to earth, there were prophets who predicted his rejection from the get-go: 'He was despised and rejected by mankind, a man of suffering, and familiar with pain' (Isaiah 53:3). Whenever you face rejection it is good to remember that Jesus knows exactly how you feel. In the Gospel of John it even says, 'If the world hates you, know that it has hated me before it hated you.' In Jesus, God has been there and done that. God understands how much it hurts to be rejected. He understands because he's been there too.

God Can Use Your Rejection

God may understand our fear of rejection, but it doesn't mean he will stop rejection from happening. And yet the Bible tells us that when it does happen God can use it for good: 'And we know that in all things God works for the good of those who love him' (Romans 8:28). In the book of James it says: 'Consider it pure joy …whenever you face trials of many kinds, because you know that the testing of your faith produces perseverance' (James 1:2). This means that in pushing into God during our times of fear it can help to strengthen our faith. Not only that, but rejection can encourage perseverance in what we are working for.

All across our culture we can see examples of people facing rejection but using this to power themselves forwards. Director Stephen Spielberg was turned down three times by one university before going on to become a hugely successful film maker. Singer Elvis Presley was told he would never amount to anything before getting a record contract and becoming the King of Rock and Roll and Anna Wintour, Editor-in-Chief of *American Vogue*, was fired from one of her first jobs! Rejection is not the end of your story; it can be a key stepping stone in moving forwards. With God working your rejection for good, why should we fear it?

God Will Never Reject You

God understands our rejection and can use our rejection, but the best thing? God will never reject us. In the Bible, Jesus promises, 'I am with you always, to the end of the age' (Matt 28:19), and Paul promises that nothing 'neither death nor life, neither angels nor demons . . . will be able to separate us from the love of God that is in Christ Jesus our Lord' (Romans 8:38–39). God has already accepted us, fully and wholeheartedly until the end of the age! Knowing that we are already accepted by God is the ultimate anti-venom to the rejection of others. We can stand fearless in the face of rejection because we have already been accepted by the only voice that truly matters.

ELIZABETH NEEP is a Commissioning Editor and Publicist for SPCK and writes fiction in her spare time. She is passionate about making faith accessible to all and breaking down stereotypes surrounding Christianity.

CASTING ALL

YOUR ANXIETIES ON HIM

BECAUSE HE

C
A
R
E

1 PETER 5:7(ESV)

F
O
R

Y
O
U

ANNA SOFIA
VASILENKO

POSITIVELY SHAPING SOCIETY X NYC

HILLSONG YOUTH X YOUNG ADULTS

FEAR OF REJECTION

"NOW I UNDERSTAND THAT SEX IS SACRED AND SAFE. WHAT I GREW UP THINKING, WHAT I WAS TAUGHT AND WHAT OUR CULTURE SAYS, AREN'T WHAT DEFINED MY BODY. INSTEAD IT'S WHAT GOD SAYS ABOUT IT. ONCE I REALIZED THAT AND STOPPED 'STRUTTING MY STUFF' OR THINKING THAT THE DYSFUNCTION OF SEX IN OUR CULTURE WAS THE NORM, I GOT LESS ATTENTION, BUT I HAD MORE ACCEPTANCE."

What does today's culture tell you about how to overcome fear and what fear is? Much of culture talks about fear as if it's a fuse, a propeller to go forward, and once you've reached that and accomplished your goal, and overcome the fear, then it's lessened or it's gone. Many speak of fear as if it's your motivation to reach that goal and overcome it, and then gain power.

But I think what culture can't and won't be able to explain is, what now? What happens after? After the goal, the power, overcoming the fear? There will always be a point, when the fear is overcome and the goal is achieved, that you think, 'What's next?' It will always bring you back to the question of eternity and you'll need Jesus for that.

How has your relationship with Jesus redefined how you view and overcome fear? My fear changed. My fear is no longer a fear of self, or rejection, but now it's more so for other people. I don't want people to walk any further without knowing true love and acceptance that is in Jesus. Hopelessness doesn't have to be your reality, and I want people to know that. My fear is that they won't. I don't want people to live like that anymore.

Where do you feel God is leading you in the future? Everywhere. I believe my call in life is to not only be an artist but more so to be an influencer of many through my art. I want to reclaim how people look at the human body from a sexual object to something God created in his image – meaning it should be beautiful and not perverted.

It's meant to be whole and majestic because he says our bodies are temples, which means they shouldn't be looked at as a sexual object, or on a scale of hot or not. The body should not bring shame. I want my art to show a balance, the body isn't something that's meant to be paraded nor meant to be hidden in shame. I want to convey the healthy median.

What advice would you give the next generation, wanting to follow a dream but feeling fearful? It might hurt but wounds heal. Look to where you're getting your ointment from, look to where you'll get your healing from. So many places and things will tell you, 'We heal, we heal,' but it can never be complete.

Above all, love heals all. Who gives love in the fullest form? Who gives in the most sacrificial form? It's always been and always will be Jesus. Rejection will come in art, in love, in New York, all over the world. We will constantly face it, and it can hurt. But if you know your healing comes from love, and you know where to go, to Jesus, then you got this.

What made you want to focus your art on the female anatomy and what rejection came with that? Growing up in New York was such a culture shock for me, having been brought up by a Russian family and taught by my grandmother. It was always such a strict way of looking at sex and the human body. I was constantly told not to think about it, talk about it, and to cover up completely. New York said the opposite.

Our culture said the opposite. Magazines, TV, my friends said the opposite. Being catcalled on the street as a kid and as a teenager said the opposite. Guys at school talking about my body said the opposite. I started to think of it as a good thing. I started to think that this was it, that this is what my body is. It's what it's for, for people to rate it and look at and talk about. But now I know that's not what God intended for it to be, and that's not what he says.

Now I understand that sex is sacred and safe. What I grew up thinking, what I was taught and what our culture says, that doesn't define my body. Instead it's what God says about it. Once I realized that and stopped 'strutting my stuff' or thinking that the dysfunction of sex in our culture was the norm, I got less attention, but I had

more acceptance. At first, it hurt. It was rejection from the world, but led to acceptance of myself. I stopped overthinking weight and clothes and makeup and I started just loving who I was. I stopped being self-conscious and insecure. I stopped working out in order to look a certain way to impress other people and instead I worked out to be healthy and have energy so I can do more and help more people. Self-acceptance was so beautiful and it made me draw closer to God. It didn't make me egotistic but it just brought me acceptance and gratitude for who I already am. I think that's what society struggles with. People feel as if they have to show and give so much in order to be loved and accepted and get 'attention'. But the love that they receive isn't love. It's moments and feelings that they are chasing. And they chase and seek these things because they don't know where to find it. They don't know true love.

Before I was afraid of speaking up about what I believe in, but through my art it's become this beautiful way to start conversations. My art raises questions and the answer to those questions always goes back to God. So now I get to use my gifts to shine light and bring people right back to love, to God.

"SO FAITH COMES FROM HEARING, AND HEARING THROUGH THE WORD OF CHRIST."

"SO FAITH COMES FROM HEARING, AND HEARING THROUGH THE WORD OF CHRIST."

ROMANS 10:17 (ESV)

ASHLEY
JOHN-BAPTISTE

"It absolutely changed my view on rejection.
I was like, God has a plan for my life and it
doesn't depend on what this group of people
have to say or what they might think."

FEAR OF REJECTION

" WHERE WERE YOU BORN?

South London. I was born into quite a vulnerable, dysfunctional home. My mum was really young and in an abusive relationship when she had me and as a result I was put into foster care. I was shunted between homes all across south London for most of my childhood but I still have some great childhood memories. My second foster home was with this amazing woman, a larger than life character – think the Big Momma from Big Momma's House – and I got on great with my foster brother. He was like my best mate, playing football around the estate.

What do you do? I'm a journalist and presenter for the BBC, producing films for a BBC News programme. I'm also a speaker, going into schools and private companies across the country, sharing my story of growing up in the care system. I try to encourage children in care to do something positive with their lives. I'm also a musician, still performing when I get the chance.

Who inspires you to be fearless and why? Denzel Washington – a man who is at the top of his craft, with all the trappings, yet he uses his platform to share his vulnerabilities, faith and uplift others. Nelson Mandela – his integrity and ability to pursue a vision with humility in the face of hostile opposition is so inspiring. I think a lot of what he did is fearlessness personified. I'm also blessed to have amazing peo-ple around me, incredible friends and people at church who encourage me to be fearless, to think big and not be de-feated by my insecurities.

What were you scared of as a child? Funnily enough, even though rejec-tion was something I lived with a lot, I was still scared of it. I think part of the reason I perform now probably stems from that childhood fear of rejection. Fears like: 'Am I good enough?' 'Am I likable?' and 'Will I be accepted?' Be-cause I was shunned so much from different people groups and families and schools, there was always that fear of, 'Is it going to happen again?' I think this weird thing happens where that fear seems to outwork itself into not caring, but actually the fear is a lot deeper. You think you're just protecting yourself, but you get a cold heart.

"It's never been, 'Follow God and everything will be perfect.' It's been, 'Follow me – it's ambiguous; follow me – it's great; follow me – I'm broke; follow me – now wait...' It's only God and his word that carry me through fear and uncertainty."

Quitting The *X Factor* – hands down! I was in a band that was put together at the boot camp stage and it was so fun. I got to perform at the O2 Arena in front of Kelly Rowland, Tulisa, Gary Barlow, Louis Walsh, and got to meet incredible culture shapers like Bruno Mars. Our group did really well on the show and made it to the live finals. Being famous and having a record contract was all within our reach. Then I quit. I just had this strong conviction that I was not where God wanted me to be and I had to be obedient to that. I continued to pray about it and God kept showing me, in the specific way he speaks to me, that I needed to leave. It wasn't what I wanted to hear! I feared the whole thing – telling my band mates, telling the show, the public rejection for giving away something everyone wanted.

Yes. I got hounded by a tabloid newspaper for weeks. I remember the week after I quit, it was a rainy Sunday night and I was getting the bus, the floor was damp, the sky was grey – worlds away from the glamour of The *X Factor*! I couldn't find my Oyster card, and then this lady behind me said, 'Well, if you stayed on the show, you wouldn't have to be getting on this bus now, would you?' I was like, 'Wow, this is the glory of following God!' I definitely didn't feel a sense of peace or understanding about the decision straightaway. I just had to be obedient, following God step by step. I knew enough about God to know I didn't need him to constantly stroke my emotions. I just had to do it. It was really hard.

Absolutely. It was two or three months after that, that BBC 3 tweeted me and asked me to do a documentary with them about growing up in care. It took a while to agree to it but when

I did an agent got in touch and told me I should be a speaker and so, within about six months of leaving the show, I am speaking to thousands of people across the country about my story.

And I didn't chase any of it. It's never been, 'Follow God and everything will be perfect.' It's been, 'Follow me – it's ambiguous; follow me – it's great; follow me – I'm broke; follow me – now wait . . .' It's only God and his word that carry me through fear and uncertainty.

Psalm 24:27. 'Even if my mother and father forsake me, the Lord will take care of me.' It's a no-brainer for someone like me. I remember a couple of years ago, just being in my bedroom having private time with God, and I just got this picture of me as a little baby on a hill, on a green meadow. The baby was enchanted by the father and even though the backdrop changed, the baby and the father stayed the same. It was like God was saying, 'I've got you. Keep your eyes on me.'

Do it afraid. I'm often in situations that push me beyond my experience, beyond what I think I'm capable of and it's important to know those feelings might not go away. I think the best advice I've been given is to do the right thing in light of how I feel and don't let feelings of fear dictate the decisions you make. Don't let the feelings of inadequacy stop you from walking into what God has for you.

I think it's the fear of looking like you've got it all together. That fear that you have to have a social media following, really good-looking friends, a really glossy lifestyle, even if you're a 15-year-old preparing to do your

GCSEs. It's ridiculous! Fear of what others think can impact the decisions we make or can even see us avoid deep relationships because we feel the pressure to be liked by everyone.

I was really fortunate that when I was fostered I lived with some Christian families. One of my placements was with a lady who lived in Peckham and she went to a Salvation Army church. At the time I hated it but there was this youth pastor who was relentless in hanging out with me and caring about me and so I began to go. Then I began to hear worship music and I just loved it. God was wooing me through it and it just felt like home.

I remember one night when I was about fourteen being in the supermarket with my foster mum. I saw a dad play fighting with his son and, even though I wasn't always like 'I don't have a dad' as a kid, something in me just imploded and I just felt an overwhelming sense of anger, hurt, pain. I got home and the kid in me just wept in my bedroom. And I remember thinking, 'God, if you're real, and you being like a dad is real, I really want it.' I felt this blanket of reassurance that God was who he said he was. I knew I was a child of God.

Once I grasped that God had a plan for my life, my behaviour just incrementally improved. It absolutely changed my view on rejection. I was like, God has a plan for my life and it doesn't depend on what this group of people have to say or what they might think. I didn't know how to explain it then, but looking back I think I grasped that there was an eternal impact to how I live today. I felt free to not be defined by limited perceptions of others, free to not be defined by what my mum did or what my dad did, and free to be who God wanted me to be.

GOD CONTINUED, "THIS IS THE SIGN OF THE COVENANT

I AM MAKING BETWEEN ME AND YOU AND EVERYTHING LIVING AROUND YOU AND EVERYONE LIVING AFTER YOU. I'M PUTTING MY RAINBOW IN THE CLOUDS, A SIGN OF THE COVENANT BETWEEN ME AND THE EARTH. FROM NOW ON, WHEN I FORM A CLOUD OVER THE EARTH AND THE RAINBOW APPEARS IN THE CLOUD, I'LL REMEMBER MY COVENANT BETWEEN ME AND YOU AND EVERYTHING LIVING, THAT NEVER AGAIN WILL FLOODWATERS DESTROY ALL LIFE. WHEN THE RAINBOW APPEARS IN THE CLOUD, I'LL SEE IT AND REMEMBER THE ETERNAL COVENANT BETWEEN GOD AND EVERYTHING LIVING, EVERY LAST LIVING CREATURE ON EARTH." GENESIS 9:14-15 (MSG)

RICH
WILKERSON JR

"At some point in life you have to discover
the simple fact that, unless you face your fear,
you'll always be back again. You'll always
be running in the opposite direction."

FEAR OF REJECTION

Rich, you were fourteen when you moved to Miami. Your parents took over leadership of Trinity Church, Miami. How did you feel moving to the city? I think at first there was this sense of excitement. I was pretty excited about it because Miami seemed so, you know, cool. But when I got there, it was very, very challenging just because I was out of my comfort zone. I'd grown up in one place, same school, same church for fourteen years, and now I'm on the other side of America. Everything about Miami is the opposite of Tacoma, Washington, not only geographically – they literally are the farthest places you can go – but then just everything about the climate, the food, the people, the culture.

And so I think it was a really, really shaping time in my life. Fourteen years of age…you're going into high school. So in my formative years I made this massive transition. Looking back now, I'm so grateful for it because I think it taught me a whole lot about adapting. It taught me about being flexible. I didn't have empathy for people. I'd feel like they were the outsider. It was the first time in my life that I was like an outsider. I didn't know anybody and so I had to learn how to make new friends. I'm grateful for it now but back then when I was in it, it was painful, it was challenging, it was super-uncomfortable. But I've learned that it's oftentimes in those spaces where you're uncomfortable that you tend to grow the most. It kind of forces you to discover some strength that you didn't know you had.

What were the initial challenges you and your parents found settling in to leading a church, a big, inner city church? I think there were, number one, just practical challenges in people groups that just think completely differently. We'd left a suburban type of primarily Caucasian-style church in Washington. And now we were in an urban inner-city church, which was really made up of lots of different people groups, lots of different nationalities, lots of different ethnicities, but primarily had a lot of the islands – Caribbean, Jamaican, Haitian – and they all just came from different places. And so a lot of, maybe, the strategies and style of how we did things before, that all practically had to change. But

> **I think, honestly, getting to know Jesus more, and discovering more about who he is, what he did, what he's done for me, and who he says that I am because of him.**

then the spiritual things were invading, I think, a dark territory. And so whenever we try to take ground for the kingdom of God and advance the local church into places like Miami and other urban cities that are not really known for thriving churches, I think there is going to always be pushback. I think the enemy, the devil, doesn't want us to win, and so I think all sorts of other kind of unforeseen, crazy things pop up. And I usually say those are spiritual things. And so I think those were some of the challenges that we were up against.

Growing up, can you relate to any of the major fears people face? I think we all deal with different types of fears and we all have different levels of fear. I think I always had a really good family. I think I knew the gospel and so the fear of death has never been something that's riddled me, if you know what I'm saying. But I don't like to think about death. It's not like I'm excited about any of that.

But I think more practical fears: being insecure, being lonely – just trying to fit in. I think junior high and high school, just discovering who you are. Sometimes just feeling like you don't fit in. And doing everything that's not really who you are to fit in. I think I had fear just to be accepted and be considered okay, cool. And so I think sometimes I made poor decisions based upon being accepted by my peers, so it was classic peer pressure.

How do you feel God helped you overcome the fears as you were growing up? I think, honestly, getting to know Jesus more, and discovering more about who he is, what he did, what he's done for me, and who he says that I am because of him. I think those are all the most practical things that helped me create good confidence. Also, I think discovering good friends. Having people in my life that really love me, not for what I can do or because of my gifts, but just because they love me. I think all those things brought security and brought strength. And I also just discovered in life that really all of God's great plans for us, all of our 'God dreams', if you will, all of our success – I don't like that word always – but all of our success is always on the other side of our fear.

So at some point in life you have to discover the simple fact that, unless you face your fear, you'll always be back again. You'll always be running in the opposite direction. And at some point you realize, 'Wow! I don't actually have to be afraid.' Whenever I sense that I'm afraid of something, it just tells me there's something great on the other side. So face it. Run through it. Deal with it. And, as you face it, you discover there's a whole beautiful world on the other side of your fear.

Do you see ways that your parents helped guide you in overcoming fears? Yeah. I think I had two parents who were massive encouragers and spoke to my potential instead of speaking to my present. I think they would speak words over me, and my dad, when we were younger, gave all his sons a word from the Lord. So my oldest brother was the child of promise. My little brother, Graham, was the child of destiny.

And I was the child of courage. That was the word that was given over me. And I remember in my bedroom, my mom had this artist come in and, next to my bed, it was like 'Child of Courage' and it had a verse. So I grew up my whole life with my parents calling me 'Child of Courage'. And I think when things like that get spoken over you, in times of need

you remember those words that they projected on your life. And I'm grateful that I had parents that projected the word 'courage' on my life so that when fear came up, I would face it.

From your parents' lives, what's the biggest challenge that they have overcome? And what did you learn from it? I don't know for sure what they would say, but I would probably guess they would say my little brother, Graham. He was born healthy but at six months of age, he was misdiagnosed with spinal meningitis, which ultimately took his life, and he was dead for over ten minutes on the doctors' table. By the grace of God, doctors revived him. We think it's a miracle. But with that, there was a major loss of oxygen to the brain. They thought he would never walk, talk, see or hear. He does all of those things, but he's had severe setbacks and challenges because of brain damage. He's an amazing guy. But I think raising a child with special needs has been a constant challenge, and probably a threat of the enemy to cast fear in their life – to say that tomorrow is going to be worse than today.

I think watching them face that fear and continue to be hopeful, continue to speak prophetically into the future that Graham was going to develop and get better and better and better, and to move into tomorrow with a hope and a belief that things can get better, I think that's great, great testimonies of who they are. So watching them live that out, and still watching them live that out, has always been a massive, massive jolt to my faith, and a massive encouragement to me to keep moving forward as well.

With all the speaking you are doing on TV shows, your books, life getting bigger and more influential, what have you learnt from mentors about dealing with the trappings that come from a big life? I think you've got to know why you're doing what you're doing. You've got to make sure you've got good voices of people around you to keep you grounded, and you've got to keep the main thing as the main thing.

So it's like knowing why, knowing who and really knowing what – which is the main thing: Jesus. Why we're doing it is because he's given us space. And who is having the right people around us constantly to keep us grounded and checking in on us. Having accountability is vital.

Over the years, you've spoken messages about overcoming fear. Can you tell us one of your favourite sermon illustrations that we could learn from? One of my favourite sermon illustrations about fear? I don't know if I can think of a great sermon illustration by me. The story of Gideon, when we're talking about fear, can always come to my mind. Here's a guy who's threshing wheat in a winepress. He's doing a real task but in the wrong place, and the reason why he's there is because he's afraid. And God calls him out of the winepress and says, 'You're going to lead this great army.' And he's pretty freaked out: 'How am I going to do this? Don't you know who I am? Yada-yada-yada…' And God says, 'I'm going to be with you,' and gives him this big army. Then God just keeps dwindling down this army to 300 men. This is the real 300, right?

And it's just a beautiful story, where God's trying to say, 'Look, if you're with me, you've got nothing to be afraid of. I'm going to take care of it.' I just like that Gideon obeyed, that he goes with him. Once again, God speaks to his potential before Gideon even walks out. He calls him a mighty man of valour or a mighty warrior. And I just think that for anyone who's reading this …that's what God says about us. Before he was a warrior, God already called him a warrior.

I like that idea that if you face the fear, you're going to see that what God says about you actually is true. But you actually have to get up out of the winepress. You actually have to obey and step out, and God will fight your battles for you and with you.

Do you have a favourite scripture that reminds you of this, when you're in a situation of starting to feel fear? Proverbs 3:5–6. 'Trust in the Lord with all your heart and lean not on your own understanding. In all your ways acknowledge him. He'll make your paths straight.' I just always liked it because it says, 'Don't lean on your own understanding.'

So don't lean on what makes sense to you. Don't lean on your natural abilities, your gifting, your talent, your strategies – trust in him. And then, when we do that, he promises to make our paths straight. It's so practical.

Do you have a personal testimony of someone in your church of standing and facing fear? I think there's so many people. Every one of our key servant leaders – volunteers – are people that, a lot of them, never thought they'd be doing what they're doing. And God's spoken to them and now they're going for it. I'm thinking about different musicians. I'm thinking about different worship leaders that were afraid to sing. The list goes on and on.

There's someone I'm thinking of right now who we asked to be a small group leader and just didn't think they were qualified to do it. They felt afraid but took the plunge anyway and went for it. And the small group right now is just dozens and dozens of people and they're totally being challenged and encouraged and finding a home in church. And it's because this person, who was kind of afraid to deal with a group of people, and didn't think they were qualified, stepped up and did it.

Being part of church life for many years, what is the greatest fear you've seen that's preventing Christians from being all that God has called them to be? I think probably the fear of rejection. The fear of failure. I think most kind of know what they're supposed to do or what they want to do, but they're just so afraid to fail. And at some point you've got to be more excited about the opportunity of winning and succeeding than you are with the fear of failing. I'd much rather try and fail than never try at all.

What do you think is important for people to understand about prayer and overcoming fear? The Bible says that God hasn't given us a spirit of fear but a spirit of love, sound mind and power. And so I think that when you pray, you're connecting with God and as God's Spirit is in you, you recognize who you are. I think prayer is vital. The more we're connecting to God, the more we're going to overcome our fear.

PASTOR RICH WILKERSON JR is a dynamic communicator with a passion to encourage and inspire this generation. Rich, and his wife DawnCheré, pastor VOUS Church in Miami. VOUS Church is a catalyst of faith, creativity and diversity that celebrates the unique culture of its vibrant city. Every June, Rich and DawnCheré host thousands of young adults at the annual VOUS Conference held at the Jackie Gleason Fillmore Theater on South Beach. He is the author of Sandcastle Kings: Meeting Jesus in a Spiritually Bankrupt World. *Rich and DawnCheré offered a peek inside their world with their docu-series,* Rich In Faith, *a 10-episode feature on the Oxygen network.*

"I think prayer is vital. The more we're connecting to God, the more we're going to overcome our fear."

GROUP DISCUSSION ✕ QUESTIONS
CHAPTER 3 FEAR OF REJECTION

Spielberg. Presley. Wintour. Three people, as Elizabeth and Dan remind us, who faced painful rejection in their early careers, but somehow managed to overcome such discouragement and rise to be known as world leaders in their respective fields. And they are not rarities: you could add to the list Albert Einstein, Walt Disney, Claude Monet, Oprah Winfrey, Michael Jordan, Steve Jobs, Bill Gates, Abraham Lincoln and J.K. Rowling. Even Greek philosopher Socrates, one of the founders of Western thought, found rejection among his contemporaries and was sentenced to death (as fate would have it, they disagreed with his pursuit of goodness and justice).

Being human, we long to be accepted and welcomed in the presence of others, which means that rejection is one of our deepest ingrained fears. Rejection seems to affirm what frightens us the most: something about us is wrong, lacking or broken. In turn, rejection makes us feel insufficient, unwanted and even unlovable. Deep within us, our subconscious is aware that rejection sits second in line in the journey that begins with ridicule – and ends with loneliness.

It is little wonder that we go to such extreme lengths to protect ourselves from rejection. Like a boxer using his gloves, hands and arms to shelter his head from a violent and relentless opponent, we draw upon every mechanism we have to guard us from the feeling of rejection. For some, this is seen in a lack of emotional, social or professional assertiveness. For others, it is expressed in clingy, obsessive or jealous behaviour in relationships. In extreme circumstances, those who fear rejection can seek harm on those they fear will reject them. Such is the negative motivational power of

rejection that it could be argued that the greater portion of human effort and endeavour is aimed at minimizing the possibility of denunciation from those around us. But let's be clear: rejection is not part of God's plan for his children. Period.

REFLECTION QUESTIONS

1. Why do we fear rejection?
2. What is it that follows rejection and terrifies us so greatly?
3. The Church is intended to be a place where the fear of rejection is not to be found. Read Ephesians 4:32. Paul instructs the Church to be kind, tender-hearted and forgiving towards one another. Why does Paul expect us to act this way? If someone were to experience this kind of community for ten, twenty or thirty years, what effect would it have on their life?
4. Our greatest fear (and for good reason) is the fear of rejection by a holy, powerful and all-knowing God. Read John 8. When the woman – who had clearly missed the mark and deserved to be rejected by the religious leaders – came before Jesus, what was his response? How does this help quell our fear of God's rejection?
5. Each of us needs welcomers who make sure that we are always welcome and wanted. Who are three people who are your welcomers? What made you think of them as welcomers?*
6. Just as others are welcomers to us and help us fight thoughts of rejection, we are also meant to be welcomers to others. Who are three people (it could be more!) that you are committed to welcoming, accepting and valuing regardless of their failures?*

* Seek out those three people that you named as welcomers to you and thank them for what they have done and how they have spoken louder than the voice of rejection. Seek out those people you are committed to welcoming and tell them in no uncertain terms that you are committed to making sure they know they are always welcome in your presence. Tell them that as long as you live, rejection will not be the loudest voice they hear!

CHAPTER 4 FEAR OF LONELINESS

"KEEP YOUR LIFE FREE FROM LOVE OF MONEY, AND BE CONTENT WITH WHAT YOU HAVE, FOR HE HAS SAID, 'I WILL NEVER LEAVE YOU NOR FORSAKE YOU.'" HEBREWS 13:5 (ESV)

FEAR OF
LONELINESS

Let me start this feature with a fairly shameless brag...
I live in the best city on the planet! London town. Yep, I
was born and raised here. I love the place. It's a global
city that fuses the best of what can be called "British"
with the best of what the whole world has to offer. The
lights never dim; the hustle never stops; there's always
a party. It's loud, creative, diverse, full of energy.
I could go on... Yet for all of the passion that I have for
this place; below the city noise is an unseen current
of loneliness. Under the connection and inclusion that
this society masquerades — when it wants to — it can
kick you to the curb of isolation.

BY: ASHLEY JOHN-BAPTISTE

This is just my personal view and it's only informed by experience, but for all of its grandeur I reckon that society in London carries a significant fear of loneliness. I think that this sense of loneliness is triggered by comparison; we compare ourselves to those Londoners who supposedly represent the high life. Social media seduces us with the cult of image and success; we question whether we will ever measure up and once the unhealthy questions begin …well, insecurity is born. That insecurity breeds the fear of loneliness, a sense that we're alone (regardless of who's around) and that we can never be truly accepted, all because we don't measure up to what society expects. Whilst this fear pervades the globe, I reckon it's way more prevalent in London.

If I'm going to keep it real in this article, I should say that the fear of loneliness is something I have struggled with in the past. At just two years old I was placed into foster care and until I was eighteen, I was shunted between foster homes and care homes. Forget about the high life of London. I was the underclass of London! With all of the family rejection I experienced as a kid, within me developed a glaring void, a void that housed dislocation and isolation. There would be times where, whether I was having dinner surrounded by a foster family or having a laugh with plenty of mates, a sunken feeling of deep isolation and despair would grip me. I was alone. If you've ever experienced the slightest form of loneliness, then I know you can relate!

As I grew up and began to grapple with my identity within wider society, loneliness was a very present fear. As I moved between phases of life and friendship groups, and came to terms with the rejection I experienced, I did for a time believe that my life would always carry this void of isolation. I believed that I'd always be lonely.

My usual way of hiding this fear was by performing and keeping up appearances. Growing up, I lived on bravado and pretending. You could have seen me as a youngster around a host of people joking and acting up, whilst on the inside I could have been detached and disengaged. My smile certainly could have been hiding the small child within who was doubtful of ever being loved and accepted. In a global city of celebrity and prosperity, I would often feel like the dejected foster kid who was without a future or a family. I feared that this would be my story for the rest of my life.

During my mid teens, however, the greatest miracle happened. I met Jesus and got baptized. With that, I began to walk a new journey of following Christ and finding my identity in him. It would, however, be a big lie to say that things worked out perfectly straightaway. In fact, my old insecurities and the baggage of being a kid in

"THAT INSECURITY BREEDS THE FEAR OF LONELINESS, A SENSE THAT WE'RE ALONE (REGARDLESS OF WHO'S AROUND) AND THAT WE CAN NEVER BE TRULY ACCEPTED, ALL BECAUSE WE DON'T MEASURE UP TO WHAT SOCIETY EXPECTS."

care clashed with my new-found faith. A big struggle for me (like so many others) was believing that God's word was applicable to my unique situation, my story.

There was a time where I assumed that if I did something wrong, the Holy Spirit would leave me; that if I ticked him off, he would just walk away and abandon me. As a result, I became a bipolar Christian – I was either very engaged with faith or completely disengaged. My approach to God was determined by my behaviour. When I was 'good' by my terms, I thought that God was present in my life; if I messed up, however, I thought that he wasn't interested in me. What a messed up way of living!

Don't get me wrong, I knew I was loved and saved, but somehow my stinging childhood experience of rejection caused me to believe on some level that God might just abandon me like the rest of my family.

I thank God that on my journey of faith, he has gone above and beyond to reassure me that he 'will never leave [me] nor forsake [me].'

A key scripture that has really empowered me to overcome the fear of loneliness is Psalm 27:10: 'Even if my mother and father forsake me, the Lord will take care of me.' In moments of fear and doubt, in those moments when I question God and his faithfulness, this scripture reassures me that my Father in heaven is always very present. Not only is he present, though, he has my back. He is on the case; He is taking care of me. This revelation of God's faithfulness and consistency in my life has demolished any fear that I am abandoned or isolated. Even on my darkest day, I know God is still taking care of me!

If you are someone who fears loneliness, please can I encourage you that you most definitely are not alone. There is a God who loves you so much, who is so obsessed with you, that he sacrificed his son Jesus to be with you. Even in those mundane and silent moments when you're alone in bed at night, God sees you and holds you.

Whilst London may be a city that can be extremely lonely, you don't have to be another victim to its seductive culture that can drop you as quick as it can pick you up in its dazzling lights. In fact, in Christ you are counter-cultural! You buck the trend! You have access to the truth that you are and always will be loved and accepted beyond measure.

Whilst it can be easy to feel the pressure to pretend and conform to others around you out of fear of loneliness, you, my friend, can stand firm in the authenticity of who you are. Why? Because you are a child of God.

If you sense that a mate or family member of yours may be living with a fear of loneliness, why not reassure them that there is a Father who will never leave them.

FOR MY FATHER AND MY MOTHER HAVE FORSAKEN ME, BUT THE LORD WILL TAKE ME IN.

PSALM 27:10 [ESV]

I have carried you
since you were born;
I have taken care of you
from your birth.
Even when you are old,
I will be the same.
Even when your hair
has turned gray,
I will take care of you.
I made you and will
take care of you.
I will carry you
and save you.

ISAIAH 46:3-4 (NCV)

JORDAN BICKNALL

POSITIVELY SHAPING SOCIETY X LONDON

HILLSONG YOUTH X YOUNG ADULTS

FEAR OF LONELINESS

Death. And I hated not being at home. I hated even going on holiday – I hated it. I was a massive homeboy. I had a fear of leaving my area.

Really? What did you think was going to happen?
I don't know. My dad has always been inclined to stay at home but he wasn't as bad as I was. I definitely had a fear of the unknown and not knowing my surroundings very well and that kind of stuff. I just didn't like going into something where I couldn't tell exactly what was going to happen. I didn't like it. I couldn't cope with it when I was younger.

Do you have a favourite book that's helped you on your spiritual journey? *For*

This I Was Born by Brian Houston. I love that book. Everyone is so individually beautiful and here for a different purpose. This is a team sport – ministry is a team sport. It's not about, 'He gets to do this,' or 'She gets to do this.' It's, 'Oh, that's so cool because we're taking the kingdom of God further,' rather than, 'Oh, it should be me doing that.' And that was a massive eye-opener for me.

How long have you been a Christian? My mum started going to church when I was five years old. At nine or ten we found a church where I really found my feet. I was playing drums every Sunday. I made some good friendships. But I wouldn't really say I had a relationship with God. I was kind of a 'Sunday

Christian', if you want to put it that way. In the first church I was at, I was actually bullied by one of the youth leaders. He used to pour stuff over me, trip me, push me. That definitely made an impression on me. I just thought, 'Well, if you're the adult and you're doing that to me, why would I want to come to church?' I got a very bad impression of what it was all about and it hindered my personal relationship with God for sure.

And then I started to hang with the wrong crowd. My mum decided to change churches to Hillsong at the time, and I never made the transition and fell out of church. And there was a four-year gap where I was not a good boy. My relationship with my parents really deteriorated. We were arguing all the time. The friends I hung out with were encouraging me to do things like under-age drinking, drugs – which I knew I didn't want to do, but I didn't know where else to go, or what else to do.

I felt so alone because I had no one to turn to. My mum would always go and talk to the youth leaders about me.

I had people who are now my best friends texting me for about three years, calling me. They never ever gave up on me.

Why did you start going to church? In that time outside of going to church I always distracted myself with other things. During exam period I let that take over. Then it was friends and Xbox and typical teenage stuff. It got to the point where that's literally all I did. I never went out. I went weeks on end without going out of the house. I didn't want that life, but I didn't have anything else. Nothing at all. And I didn't have the confidence or the sense of what else there was to go out and find… something else.

In my late teens this behaviour kind of came to a head when my cousin got involved with this girl. So she would hang around with me and him a lot. We would see each other all the time. They were the only people I would associate with. And then, all of a sudden, she said something to him about me saying me and her should hang out without him. We ended up falling out over it big time. I went to another friend's twentieth birthday because I felt I had to, and my cousin turned up that night with five of his friends to try and beat me up. It just so happened that I had gone out to get food when he arrived and my friend called to warn me not to come back. We haven't spoken since.

At that point I woke up and thought, 'What the hell am I doing? What's this all about?' And so I pulled myself together and started working harder at college, getting more involved in football, but in the back of my head there was always like, 'There must be something more. There must be something more.' Then I got a call from my mum telling me my sister's youth leader had randomly bought me a ticket to the first night of Hillsong Conference. At first I said I didn't want to go and then on the night out of nowhere something in me was like, 'You need to go.' Obviously now I know it was God. It was just this thing in me – this fear of going into the unknown – it just went away, and it was like, 'This is something you need to do, and you need to do this for yourself.'

I remember the night so vividly. I was sitting next to someone who is now one of my best friends, and Brian spoke a message of faith and then asked us if we wanted to follow Jesus and I put my hand up and burst out crying. I've never felt anything like it. I was on my knees. It was just like four years of hurt and pain all coming out. My mum was in tears because she could not believe it. My sister could not believe it. Because it had been such a journey for me – everything I'd been through. And me beating myself up had been the cause of a lot of that pain, me not feeling like I deserved anything or deserved to be treated any better. And it was just that real moment of love and peace that came over me that night. I've never looked back since.

What happened after Conference then, in terms of your relationship with God? It wasn't an instant thing. It took time. I started to come to church a bit and build relationships with people. So I started embedding. That's what I love about the Church. I love the statement that says, 'You can belong before you believe.' That was everything to me, because I actually felt that I had some kind of belonging, even though I wasn't there all the time. Because if you've felt that you have nothing to tie yourself to, you don't feel like you have a cause or a purpose. And when I heard that phrase I thought, 'Wow, some people actually cared.' And they'd tried to do it for three years, but I was just at the stage where I was never interested or never realized what they were trying to do.

Why do you think so many young people feel like they don't belong, or experience feelings of worthlessness, of loneliness, of not being able to be authentic because they want to be accepted? I feel like a lot of it is caused by social media. I was reading something the other day that social media is the biggest cause of body-shaming and social discrimination in the world. Because it's all filters. It's all highlights. It's not the real problems of everyday life. I know from experience, you think that's real life, and you think that this life people portray on social media – portrayed to you – is real. But it's so not.

So tell us a bit about Reggie Dabbs? Reggie Dabbs is, according to CNN, the number one communicator to teenagers in the world. He comes with this incredible story of love and peace and togetherness that's all come from his upbringing. His story begins with his mum sleeping with someone for twenty quid to buy a dinner for her other three kids. That's how he was made.

"I JUST DIDN'T LIKE GOING INTO SOMETHING WHERE I COULDN'T TELL EXACTLY WHAT WAS GOING TO HAPPEN. I DIDN'T LIKE IT. I COULDN'T COPE WITH IT WHEN I WAS YOUNGER."

And his mum actually gave him away to her favourite school teacher at the time. He didn't know this until he went to a parent–teacher evening, and he realized that his parents were both a lot older than his friends' parents. And he asked them, 'Why are you older?' And they sat him down and said. 'We're not your real parents. Your mum gave you away but kept your brothers and your sister.' From the ages of eight to 21, he wanted to die. And that is his message – that he's not 21 anymore. He's not that person anymore, and that's because he's got God in his life.

Jesus has given him this incredible calling and anointing to go out and speak to one and a half million kids a year face to face, all around the world, and just say Jesus loves them. The amount of kids who have just run out crying is crazy. Even three weeks ago, it happened five or six times in one school, in one assembly. Even when you watch them walk in, you can see it in their faces. They're trying to be this person they're not, and I know how that feels – this longing for acceptance and belonging to society, to your friendship group, to your parents, to your teachers, to your family… whoever. There's this such desperate longing for

acceptance that's created in our current society. And it's just sad. And I will now, being in the position I am, not sit still and watch it happen. I want to do something about it. And that's for me the reason I love what I'm doing.

What advice would you offer to someone saying, 'I'm struggling with this feeling of loneliness. I've got a lot of people around me but you can still feel really lonely'?
I think there's a massive difference between having people around and letting people in. So my advice would be to let one person in. Speak to someone that you know you can confide in. Even if you don't get the advice you want, you'll feel so much better just to get it out. Because when all these thoughts are bouncing around in your head, that's all they're doing if you don't speak to someone. So don't think, 'Oh, I've got all these people around me,' because actually it's pointless having people around you if you're not letting people in. Parents can often be a safe bet, but it's very difficult for parents at times because they're not involved in your social circles, your society, your day-to-day life.

So it's finding the right person. That is the ultimate challenge. That's the real challenge. But I think that's

almost a challenge for us to also be that person for the people in our lives. That's my conviction now, that I am always going to be that person for whoever is in my life. I've had boys come to me with stuff, which is the most amazing thing because the one thing I said to God and said to myself was, 'If I'm going to do this, I'm going to be that person that wasn't there for me.' That's why I do what I do.

Do you have any dreams for youth at church? Schools hold the key to society, because that's where all the young people are in one place. So we're trying to put some school programmes together. We've got one for girls called Shine, and we've got quite a few schools that we're looking to take that into this year. We're putting together some stuff to do with boys in schools – Strength. And there's a leadership one we're working on as well. Just to take that message into schools because it's so difficult to get people through the doors in church nowadays, because there's this thing that religion is mainstream. But Jesus isn't mainstream. Jesus didn't bring religion, he brought relationship, he brought love, he brought peace. He brought everything and took away the religious side of it.

"BECAUSE THE ONE THING I SAID TO GOD AND SAID TO MYSELF WAS, 'IF I'M GOING TO DO THIS, I'M GOING TO BE THAT PERSON THAT WASN'T THERE FOR ME.' THAT'S WHY I DO WHAT I DO."

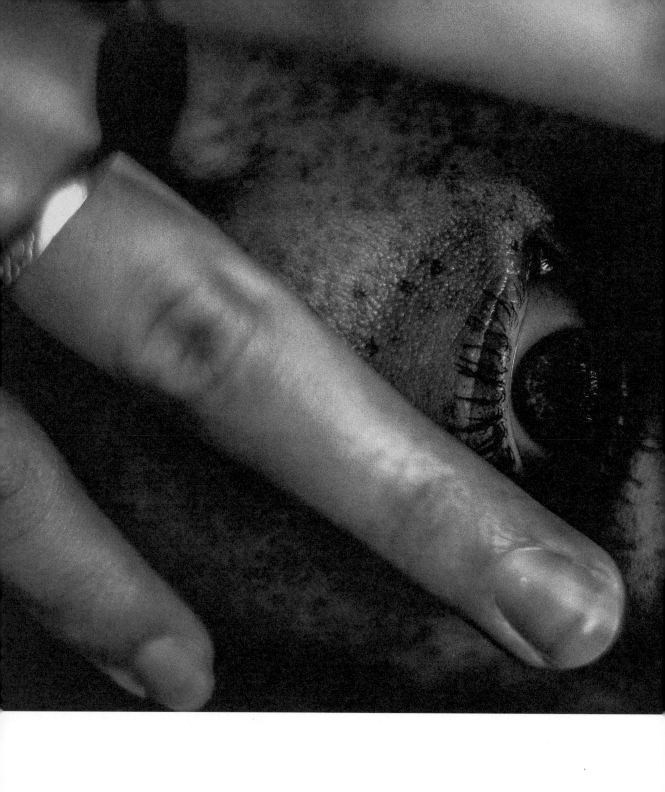

It's in Christ that we find out who we are and what we are living for. Long before we first heard of Christ and got our hopes up, he had his eye on us, had designs on us for glorious living, part of the overall purpose he is working out in everything and everyone.

EPHESIANS 1:11-12 (MSG)

CHERYL
FAGAN

"I often say sex cannot be used as an exchange –
for example, to keep a partner or for your self-worth.
It can't be used to fill a void. Sex may feel like an instant
gratification to fill the void of loneliness, but sex was not
designed to be used that way. This does not honour
yourself or the other person."

FEAR OF LONELINESS

Where were you born?
Sacramento, California

What do you do?
I am a sex educator.

What hobbies do you have?
Cafés and the beach!

Who inspires you to be fearless and why?
Martin Luther King Jr. He literally died for the cause. He demonstrates that people and human rights are worth the fight.

What were you scared of as a child? Being alone.

What's the biggest risk you've taken? Leaving my family in California to move to Sydney, Australia.

Do you have any key verses you live by to overcome fear? 'When I am afraid, I put my trust in you.' Psalm 56:3. We don't need to understand, but choose to trust.

Have you ever received any advice about overcoming fear? To paraphrase the words of Hillsong Pastor Robert Fergusson: let your fire – your passion for something – fuel you to overcome the fear.

Do you have a favourite book that's helped you on your spiritual journey? *The Pursuit of God* by A.W. Tozer

What personal experiences growing up can you share about loneliness and the fear of being lonely? My mother had me and my older brother around nineteen years old. My biological father was abusive, so my mom had to separate us from him when I was three – I actually didn't meet him until I was seventeen. She started dating my step-dad when I was six. My mom was everything to me. I was so afraid of losing her or not having her attention, given my experience of an absent father. Growing up I often felt lonely and misunderstood.

What was the tipping point for you writing your book about sex, *On Top*? I had recently moved from Sacramento to Sydney and I had connected with a couple of younger teenage girls who I started to mentor. One day we met up and they brought a few friends, all aged between fourteen and seventeen, who like many teenagers had uncountable questions regarding sex, dating, boys and relationships. This was a safe and shame-free space where they could ask anything they wanted, and they did. We decided we would meet every couple of months to foster that conversation, yet we always went over time and I felt they needed to go deeper internally.

I decided I would create a simple PDF guide with questions they could take home and study on their own. This turned into two years of research and writing. I saw the gap between school sex education, the lack of conversation within the home and silence in most churches. I discovered a passion to normalize the conversation so that young people would be empowered to make healthy choices.

What feedback have you received from this? Have you learnt anything from their responses to it? The positive feedback has been overwhelming. From teens, to young adults, to parents, people have thanked me for being brave and talking about something that is not normally talked about. When something isn't talked about it creates shame and guilt, and often we are questioning the same things, so why not be open, vulnerable and seek answers?

What do you think secular culture offers youth in terms of an antidote to loneliness? Secular culture sells the narrative to youth that the cure to loneliness is found in a relationship, and that the ultimate way to express love in a relationship is sex. Sex has therefore become many people's antidote to loneliness. Also, being single can be confusing and there is often a lot of pressure inside and outside the church to be in a relationship. This can lead to misusing relationships and people to fill a void of loneliness rather than finding genuine connection and fulfilment.

"It's clear throughout the Bible that God's plan for sex was to bring pleasure amongst both partners and this creates unity in marriage. When faced with a sexual choice, ask yourself, how does this honour myself? How does this honour the other person? How does this honour God? What I want you to think about it, is how you treat others. Our choices impact others. As Christians it's not about being uptight, but respecting ourselves and others and being kind – it's the golden rule!"

What is God's antidote to loneliness? The story of God and humanity is one of inclusiveness and acceptance. Loneliness is the lie. God is always with us and waiting for you to turn to him and seek him. He wants you to tell him your fears and anxieties, so he can show you how much he cares!

Where do you think churches get it wrong when they try to talk about sex, especially to their young adults? Unfortunately, the majority of churches fail to educate and encourage healthy sexuality by simply not talking about it at all. A common experience for many and their questions about sex has been being silenced, which ends up doing more harm than good. And then when it is mentioned, it's talked about in a dirty way – until you're married, then sex is all of a sudden good.

The truth is that God created us as sexual beings. For most people, puberty is the onset of sexual feelings and desires. This is natural, so we need to talk about it and see what God's plan and purpose for sex was. As a Christian, being sex positive is embracing our sexual nature, while honouring God with our choices. This does not mean ignoring it. If we ignore it, that makes people feel dirty and sinful. Open conversations will help people to make healthy choices.

Is there a difference between desire and lust? This is a great question because so often in church when sexual desire is discussed, it's talked about in a negative way like lust or temptation to sin. As I said before, God created us as sexual beings. He knows we have sexual desires. I read once, 'It's as if Christians believe God created the entire body and the devil slapped on the genitals.' Isn't this so true? If you believe God is the creator, then you have to believe and educate yourself on yourself, your sexual body!

So there are normal sexual desires, but lust is more of a selfish, overpowering sexual desire that aims to fulfil the person's own need, not caring about the other. Lust has an 'it's all about me' attitude. It's clear throughout the Bible that God's plan for sex was to bring pleasure amongst both partners and this creates unity in marriage.

When faced with a sexual choice, ask yourself, how does this honour myself? How does this honour the other person? How does this honour God? What I want you to think about it, is how you treat others. Our choices impact others. As Christians it's not about being uptight, but respecting ourselves and others and being kind – it's the golden rule!

Are relationships important for our overall happiness? Intimacy and true connection with others is a human need. We were created for connection. Did you know that many important studies have been done to understand human connection and attachment from birth? As humans we need it not only to thrive, but to survive!

How do you know if you're only dating or hanging out with someone because you're lonely and bored or actually really into them? You're really into someone when you tend to think about them often, get excited to see them, want to learn more about them and introduce them to your friends. Is there something special or unique to spending time with this person compared to others? Make a list of what you like about this person. This can help determine your motivations for being with this person.

Does sex cure loneliness? I often say sex cannot be used as an exchange – for example, to keep a partner or for your self-worth. It can't be used to fill a void. Sex may feel like an instant gratification to fill the void of loneliness, but sex was not designed to be used that way. This does not honour yourself or the other person.

If I don't have sex I feel rejected by my peers. What should I do? Firstly, don't put your values on other people. If you do that, hopefully your friends won't do it back. Be honest and speak confidently. People always respect and admire that, even if they have a different opinion.

How can I handle rejection? Rejection is not fun. I believe it is important to keep a big-picture perspective. Not every relationship works out. After a breakup or rejection, ask yourself why you feel sad, what you can learn from the situation. Choose to believe that God has something better for you (and for that other person).

I don't want to have sex, but my partner does. How can I navigate the different values we have without rejecting them? First of all, you need to be honest and tell them how you feel about your convictions. And if they have good character they will respect that and try to understand more. I have experienced this before and I explained that my feelings for them could be expressed in different ways than just physical and I wanted to explore that. Most of the time that was respected, but if they kept pushing I knew they didn't really care about me or my thoughts and feelings, so they got the flick. It's important for your sake that the choices you make empower you rather than pressure you.

The God who made the world and everything in it, this Master of sky and land, doesn't live in custom-made shrines or need the human race to run errands for him, as if he couldn't take care of himself. He makes the creatures; the creatures don't make him. Starting from scratch, he made the entire human race and made the earth hospitable, with plenty of time and space for living so we could seek after God, and not just grope around in the dark but actually find him. He doesn't play hide-and-seek with us. He's not remote; he's near. We live and move in him, can't get away from him! One of your poets said it well: 'We're the God-created.' Well, if we are the God-created, it doesn't make a lot of sense to think we could hire a sculptor to chisel a god out of stone for us, does it?

ACTS 17:26-29 [MSG]

CHELSEA
SMITH

What's your full name?
Chelsea Rene Smith. Rene is R-E-N-E, spelt the French masculine way. And oddly enough my maiden name was also Smith, and then I married a Smith!

Where were you born?
I was born in Portland, Oregon, in the northwest part of the United States.

What do you do?
I'm a leading pastor of Churchome.

What hobbies do you have?
I am a nerd. I like to read, I love to hike and walk outside. I also like watching TV shows and playing with my kids.

Is there a particular person or people who inspire you to be fearless?
Growing up I was always inspired by Mother Teresa. Probably a very typical

answer, but what I loved was her willingness to not be comfortable, to set aside her own comfort for the sake of what she felt called to do. Also, Martin Luther King Jr and his fearlessness to go against the status quo for what he knew was right. And on a daily level, not to sound cheesy, but my husband. Just watching him in everything that he does I'm thinking, 'Wow, he's a hero.'

Were you scared of anything as a child?
I was a pretty fearless child actually. Our house got broken into almost annually and you'd think that would cause fear. But as a result, because we were still protected, I just honestly wasn't afraid of anything.

It's interesting now having an eight-year-old daughter who is so afraid

of being in a room by herself. We've told her that she's going to have to start sleeping in her own room, but as a mom who never felt like that I never know how much to push her.

So what do you feel has been the biggest risk you've taken, maybe recently or over the last few years?
I feel like my life has been a risk! I do not have a normal life. I think it's scary when you do something for the first time. So the first time I had to trust God in a meaningful, personal way I was probably nineteen and I had this boy who I thought was the one for me. He wanted to make the relationship more serious, and this was way back in the late 90s, so I said, 'If you want to be more serious, you have to ask my dad.' So he asked, and my dad just said, 'No,

"Also, Martin Luther King Jr and his fearlessness to go against the status quo for what he knew was right."

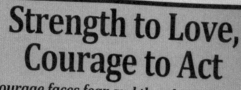

Strength to Love, Courage to Act

"Courage faces fear and thereby masters it"

Dr. Martin Luther King, Jr.

THE 38TH ANNUAL MARTIN LUTHER KING, JR. MEMORIAL MARCH

Raleigh, North Carolina
January 15, 2018 • 11 AM
State Capitol, Downtown Raleigh

SPONSORED BY: THE TRIANGLE MARTIN LUTHER KING, JR. COMMITTEE
SPONSORED PARTNER: XI MU MU CHAPTER, OMEGA PSI PHI FRATERNITY, INC.

P.O. Box 25866, Raleigh, NC 27611 • www.trianglemlk.com

you're not the man for my daughter. And, in fact, I don't think it's comfortable for you guys to be friends anymore.'

The risk (for me) was, do I do what my heart wants or do I do what I feel like I should do, which is listen to my dad? I trusted God through listening to my dad and took the risk.

Do you have a key verse that you live by to overcome fear? My favourite verse is Romans 8:28: 'We know that all things work together for good.' The reason that helped me through fear is realizing that I don't have to be afraid of anything. Good things happen, great.

Something happens that doesn't seem to be working out the way that I thought it should, then God's got it. He's going to work it out for good. And just the trust that develops.

Have you ever received any really great advice about overcoming fear? I went to Bible college straight after high school and we had a guest speaker visiting our church and as the woman was speaking, she said, 'I made a promise to God that I would never say no to anything he asked me to do because of fear.' And I was there as an eighteen-year-old and something in that just registered and I was like, 'Okay, I can do that. God, I promise I will never say no to anything that's asked of me just because I'm afraid to do it.' And that woman ended up being Judah's mom, so she's now my mother-in-law which is cool. But I've watched her live that out and I've tried to live that out myself.

Do you have a favourite book that's helped you when you need a reminder of your faith, your strength and encouragement? Back in my late teens somebody gave me a little book called *A Tale of Three Kings* [by Gene Edwards]. It's a story about Saul, David and Absalom. The premise is, there was a call on David's life. Saul, who was a lousy king, tried to take that away from him. But there is no person on earth who can take away the call of God. That's always grounded me. It means I don't have to be afraid. No human can keep us from what God has destined us for.

You're meeting people all the time across the church. What are the biggest fears that you are coming across? There is such a fear that I'm going to be insignificant, that my life isn't going to matter and I'm not going to do anything that makes a difference. It's just such a real cry of the human heart: 'Is my life going to matter?'

Does social media and the comparison that breeds make it harder? I'm a 39-year-old grown woman with three beautiful kids and I feel like I have a pretty good life. Yet there's still a good amount of times where I have to put my phone down because I'm realizing social media is making me feel unfulfilled. I usually look at social media once a week so if it's having this kind of impact on my emotions, what's it doing to sixteen-year-old girls wondering who they are and whether their lives are going to matter?

What do you think you have learnt about loneliness and why we fear it? Loneliness is one of the base fears of humanity, whether you live in Africa or America, in a skyscraper or a village. And when I look to the Bible and the creation story in Genesis, I think that makes sense. We read there that God creates everything in the world and says it's good. He creates man, and he is good. But then we get the first 'not good' in the Bible, and this is before sin has entered the picture. God says, 'It is not good for man to be alone.' Christians will so often say the cure for loneliness is the presence of God, and that's

> **The cure for loneliness isn't just being around a bunch of people. It's being with people who know the real you, your weaknesses and shortcomings.**

partly true. And yet, here we see Adam in the full presence of God, no sin, and it's still 'not good' for him to be alone. He still had a need for human connection. I think the antidote to loneliness is to be known and to know somebody else, and that's a two-way street.

We often think being alone and loneliness are the same thing, but so often in the Bible we see Jesus being alone but never being lonely. We need to not be scared of being alone but acknowledge our need for human connection at the same time.

What impacts of loneliness do you see affecting young people today? You can't talk about loneliness today without talking about social media. We filter everything and present ourselves as completely 'together' which can lead to loneliness, because the cry of our heart is actually to be known for who we are. The cure for loneliness isn't just being around a bunch of people. It's being with people who know the real you, your weaknesses and shortcomings. Then there's looking at other people's 'perfect' lives, which makes us think we're the only ones with shortcomings. That leads to such a horrific place of isolation because then we are never going to open up and allow anybody to see the real us.

Do you think church culture facilitates that? How would you describe it to someone who isn't in it? Our theology should shape our culture and so because our theology is that God accepts us, loves us and died for us, while we're still sinners, that shapes everything. Our culture is therefore one that says before you ever behave, before you ever believe, you belong. Everybody belongs no matter what you look like, or your

> ## "It's interesting to me that it was in a moment of making a mistake that I felt like God spoke to me, saying, 'I love you no matter what you do'."

background. No matter what you're walking through, you belong at church. The whole mentality where people won't come to church because they're not good enough couldn't be further from the truth. Nobody is good enough and everybody gets to belong before you do anything to earn it.

How would you describe youth culture more generally? When I think of youth culture more generally I very much see a group of kids, a group of teenagers, a group online, that says, 'If you conform to me I will accept you. If you want to dress the same way or if you want to play basketball the way I play basketball or if you conform to our values or whatever the group values are, then I will accept you.' It can seem so easy but it's so detrimental because we end up having teenagers really changing who they are and who God made them to be, in order to be accepted, in order to avoid being lonely. But as I have mentioned, it is not enough to be accepted for who we have made ourselves to be; we want people to accept who God made us to be. We want to be accepted for the real us, but what secular culture says is that you have to change who you are to be accepted. That is a horrific route to cure loneliness because you know you'll feel better for a second but it's not actually going to cure your loneliness long term.

How do you feel about that pressure to conform, particularly in relation to sex, as so often people think that is the answer to loneliness? The difference between a boy and a girl when it comes to that is crazy. It's sad that particularly for women there's so much value that comes from our sexuality and our outer appearance. I believe as Christians, as fathers, as mothers, as pastors, our job isn't to say, 'That's bad.' Our job is to add so much value for who we all are in

Christ that you don't need the value from the sexual attraction and approval of others.

Can you tell us about a time in your life where you were gripped by fear and how you overcame it? I know I said I promised I'd never say no because of fear, but I haven't been 100 percent on that. When Judah and I first started dating he was preaching here and there at little churches, and I went along with him to this high school gymnasium to hear him preach. He turned around to me and said, 'Hey, do you have anything that you want to share?' Wanting to impress my boyfriend I gave a 'spiritual' answer and said, 'Let me pray about it.' God put a scripture on my heart, and later when Judah asked me if God had said anything I just said 'Nope,' because I feared what he and the other three or four hundred students might think. A girl came up to Judah a few minutes later and said, 'Hey, I have a verse that I want to say tonight.' And she gets up and shares the exact same verse that God had put in my heart to share but I didn't because of fear. I went home and had a restless night's sleep and woke up the next morning and began praying, 'God, I can't believe I said no. I can't believe you had to let somebody else in.'

I've never had a lot of visions in my life, but it was probably the closest thing to a vision I've ever had, when I felt the most intense love of God that I had ever felt up to that point. It's interesting to me that it was in a moment of making a mistake that I felt like God spoke to me, saying, 'I love you no matter what you do. You are mine, and nothing can change that.' This is when I realized I had a choice to make: 'Here's what your life can be like if you're isolated because of fear, or here is what you can see if you will say yes to me whatever I ask you to do and step out regardless of fear.'

I just sat there with God in that moment and said, 'Okay, God, I choose that because it's not about me.' I knew that God would have kept giving me those two options and that I didn't have to choose it in that moment. He gives options in the context of love and value and if I hadn't felt so loved and so valued by God, not for anything that I had or hadn't done, but because I was his daughter and he loved me, it would not have nearly been as easy to say yes to God for the rest of my life. What's amazing is that once we receive that value and love from God, we love and we value other people, and it is so easy to say yes even at the risk of our own fear.

CHELSEA SMITH is the co-lead pastor of Churchome in Seattle, Washington. She and her husband, Judah Smith, lead a thriving multi-site congregation with locations throughout the greater Seattle area and Los Angeles. She is a gifted leader and speaker who is passionate about the message of Jesus. Her ministry is noted for down-to-earth wisdom, authenticity, and strong faith. Judah and Chelsea have three children: Zion, Eliott, and Grace.

GROUP DISCUSSION X QUESTIONS
CHAPTER 4 FEAR OF LONELINESS

Ashley's story of loneliness, despite living in a city of millions, is a familiar tale. It's not uncommon to feel alone and isolated even when we are physically surrounded by crowds. We all experience times of being alone, and often this can be a time of positive personal, emotional and spiritual recharging. But true loneliness (or autophobia, as psychologists call it) is a deeply painful emotional state, where we can feel disconnected, alienated and isolated from others. We lack the meaningful human contact with others that brings us connection, joy and help.

When we explore the meaning of loneliness even further, we realize that it is less about proximity to people and more about access to assistance. Deep-seated loneliness is the feeling of having no one to call upon for help. It is the dreaded fear that in our time of need – social, practical, emotional, financial – we will find no one willing to come to our side. We will be alone. We will be vulnerable. And we will have to face the fight by ourselves.

The fear of loneliness often stems from a prior instance of abandonment by someone important in our lives. For Ashley, it was his parents when he was just two years old. For others, it might be a spouse that deserted them or a friend who left them to fend for themselves.

There are times in all of our lives when we need to look to others to help us, and when that help doesn't come – when we are left alone to

fend for ourselves – a deep sense of loneliness can embed itself into us, subtly influencing our choices and eating away at our lives.

The good news is that God – who designed us and knows how to bring out the best in us – wants for us to overcome the fear of loneliness, and because of that he has a plan for each of us to break free of this dreadful fear.

REFLECTION QUESTIONS

1. What is the difference between being alone and being lonely?

2. What is the root fear behind loneliness and what life events may have caused it to take hold?

3. God has given us two powerful weapons against loneliness. Read Genesis 2:15-18. What was God's first solution to Adam's loneliness?

4. How does the promise of Hebrews 13: 5-6 help you fight the fear of loneliness?

5. Each of us needs a helper, or helpers, to help us in our times of need. Who are three people who are your helpers? What made you think of them as helpers?*

6. Just as others are helpers to us and help us keep loneliness at bay, we are also helpers to others. Who are three people (it could be more!) that you are committed to helping, to standing alongside and fighting the good fight?*

* Seek out those three people that you named as helpers to you, and thank them for what they have done and how they have helped you. Seek out those people you are committed to helping and tell them in no uncertain terms that you are committed to standing by them and being their help in times of need. Tell them that as long as you live, loneliness need not be a part of their lives!

CHAPTER 5 FEAR OF DEATH

"FIGHT THE GOOD FIGHT OF THE FAITH. TAKE HOLD OF THE ETERNAL LIFE TO WHICH YOU WERE CALLED AND ABOUT WHICH YOU MADE THE GOOD CONFESSION IN THE PRESENCE OF MANY WITNESSES." 1 TIMOTHY 6:12 (ESV)

FEAR OF
DEATH

EACH HALLOWEEN, MILLIONS OF PEOPLE HIT
THE STREETS DRESSED AS GHOSTS AND ZOMBIES.
EVERY MONTH, A NEW DOCUMENTARY LIKE *MAKING
A MURDERER* IS RELEASED. IT SEEMS THAT DEATH
FROM A DISTANCE IS KIND OF FASCINATING.
BUT ZOOM IN A LITTLE CLOSER AND IT'S EASY
TO SEE HOW MANY OF US ACTUALLY FEAR IT.

BY: ELIZABETH NEEP

A family member goes to the hospital to get a lump checked – could it be cancer? A friend loses someone special and we can't bring ourselves to actually say the word – sorry for your 'loss'. If we're honest, many of us fear death. The ironic thing is, only when we let go of that fear can we truly start living. But how do we do that?

Death is Not the End

If you've ever stepped foot in church or spoken to a Christian, you'll probably know that much of what the Bible says is counter-cultural. What the Bible says about death is certainly no exception. Where our human nature fears it, the Bible embraces it! In the Bible, God shows us through his son, Jesus, that death is not the end; it is actually just the beginning.

In Genesis, the first book in the Bible tells us that God created life – all of it – the earth, the birds, the animals, man and woman. When humans decided to ignore God's commands and go their own way, sin and death came into the world. This was never part of God's plan but it did not take God by surprise. He is all-powerful and all-knowing and nothing surprises him. God always knew we would go our own way and always had a plan to draw us back to himself once and for all.

First, he needed to show us the way. If a human tried to show an ant the way to go, the ants wouldn't understand. Ants only follow ants. In the same way God sent a human to earth, to walk alongside us, to speak like we speak, to laugh like we laugh, to cry like we cry, so that we would know how to follow him, so that we would know the way.

Before Jesus came to earth, people would sacrifice an animal to God as the wage for sin. But because we are human, we'd just go on sinning again and again. God knew in order to defeat sin for good, he'd need a really, really big sacrifice. So he sent his son to die on a cross as the ultimate sacrifice for sin. Because of Jesus's death, normal people were no longer bound by sin and death: in Jesus the world was finally free.

But the best bit? Death could not hold him. On the third day after Jesus was put to death on the cross, he rose again, was seen walking and talking with his disciples and other eye witnesses, before returning to dwell with God in heaven. You can check the history books on this one, all the evidence is there – the kind that has led leading scholars to turn away from their atheist views and embrace God entirely!

In short, God chose life; humans chose death; so God chose death so that humans could chose life. Pretty cool, right? The Bible tells us that 'God's grace has now been revealed through the appearing of our Saviour, Christ Jesus, who has destroyed death and has brought life and immortality to light through the gospel' (2 Timothy 1:10).

"IN SHORT, GOD CHOSE LIFE; HUMANS CHOSE DEATH; SO GOD CHOSE DEATH SO THAT HUMANS COULD CHOSE LIFE."

Now, I have to admit, I find heaven hard to get my head around. Some of my friends who don't believe in God have said to me, 'You only believe in God because you want to believe in heaven.' For me, this couldn't be further from the truth. I believe in God because I have experienced him and his goodness in the here and now. I only believe in heaven because I believe in God's promises. So if you find heaven hard to comprehend, don't worry – I'm with you. But the Bible is pretty certain about this: because of Jesus's death, eternity is real. It also says that we won't go up to heaven and dance around on clouds, but that heaven will come down to earth and all things will be made new – not brand new, but restored, the way they were intended to be. One day, 'God will wipe every tear from their eyes, there will be no more death, or mourning or crying or pain, for the old order of things has passed away' (Revelation 21:4). Now, if that isn't Good News I don't know what is.

Death is New Life

We can see, therefore, that not only does the Bible tell us not to fear death – but that we should be expectant for it. In one of the Apostle Paul's letters, to the Church in Rome, he shares how we who believe in God, 'who have the firstfruits of the Spirit, groan inwardly as we wait eagerly for our adoption as sons, the redemption of our bodies' (Romans 8:23). If you've ever had a sick relative, or a grandparent or relative die, or watched a terrorist attack on the news, something inside you will be offended, something inside you will know it's not right, that things in this world were not as they were intended to be. And you'd be right! That is the Spirit at work inside all of us, longing for our return to the way things were intended to be. We can be fearless of death because for Christians, death will mean new life.

Death is Not Now

After the past few paragraphs, you'd be forgiven for asking, 'Isn't it just better to die now then?' – especially if you're going through a hard time and the hope of heaven seems miles away! My answer to that (thankfully backed up by the Bible!) would be, 'Heck, no!' Death is not to be feared, death is to be expected and heaven is to be anticipated, but we are not the ones to decide when our number is up (and

"THROUGH JESUS'S DEATH AND RESURRECTION, PEOPLE WHO FOLLOW JESUS WILL SHARE IN HIS RESURRECTION."

thank God for that!) As broken as this world is, it is still full of life and beauty and every day we have on this earth is a gift. Do not waste it!

When Jesus died, the war over death was won. But the battle here on earth continues. This means we live in a bit of tension – between the world as it is now and the coming of God's kingdom. Now, it should be noted that God's kingdom is not a physical place but is anywhere and anytime where God's goodness and grace and peace can be experienced here on earth. A sick child is prayed for and stays sick – we still exist in an imperfect world. A sick child is prayed for and gets well? That's God's kingdom breaking through. We exist in a middle ground. We live in the now and the not yet of God making all things new.

Die to Self

Through Jesus's death and resurrection, people who follow Jesus will share in his resurrection. Jesus promises a new life, but not just an eternal life when heaven touches earth, but a new life that starts now, today. In order for there to be a new life, there needs to be an old death – not a literal death, but a dying of our self with our old ways and a rebirth into a new self, with Christ as the centre. In Paul's letter to the Church in Rome, he explains, 'For we know that our old self was crucified with him so that the body ruled by sin might be done away with, that we should no longer be slaves to sin – because anyone who has died has been set free from sin.'

Now, notice how the Bible doesn't say we will never sin – we're human, of

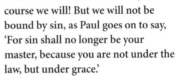

course we will! But we will not be bound by sin, as Paul goes on to say, 'For sin shall no longer be your master, because you are not under the law, but under grace.'

Though much of society fear death – both physical death and the death of idols such as money and power – if we trust God we know there is nothing to fear. Because of Jesus's death and resurrection, physical death means being with God for eternity. And today, turning away from or 'dying' to our own wants, means turning to a new life with Jesus: a life of adventure, generosity, love, kindness, peace and joy – a life of living fearlessly.

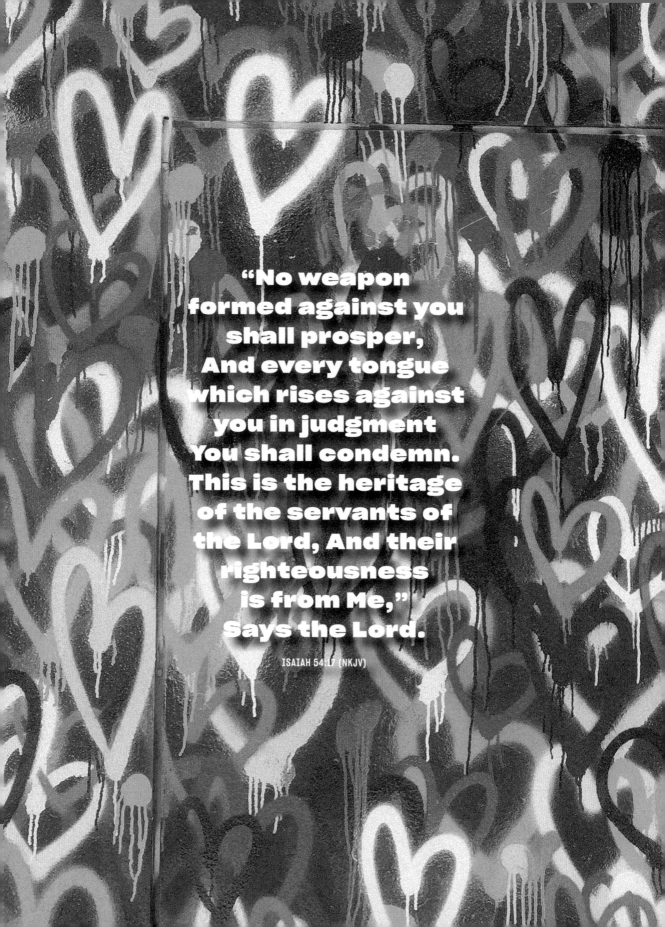

"No weapon formed against you shall prosper, And every tongue which rises against you in judgment You shall condemn. This is the heritage of the servants of the Lord, And their righteousness is from Me," Says the Lord.

ISAIAH 54:17 (NKJV)

CARINE
HARB

FEAR OF DEATH

Ever since I was a child, the fear of death gripped me. I was born in Lebanon, in the city of Beirut. My siblings and I were exposed to violence from a young age due to the ongoing war between Israel, Syria and Iran. My older cousins found this exciting. They'd hear gun sounds and watch bombs being thrown from their balconies; they were desensitized to death. The adults around me would use the war as a way of bribing me into behaving; they would tell me that 'Israel is attacking and will bomb our house' if I didn't behave. Because of this, I was constantly tormented with nightmares of dying, spending the first years of my childhood hiding under my bed.

I was five years old when I saw a dead body on the street, a young man lying in the road, under our flat, with blood covering his face. My two older brothers and my mum looked at the body and continued with their conversation. I began to believe that death was a plague that would soon reach me. I questioned the value of life because I feared dying, forbidding myself from believing that life was important because death was around the corner.

The violent culture surrounding me at the time continued to water this fear. At school in Lebanon, the teachers would pull my hair and punch me. If I dared to talk back, or ask a question out of curiosity, the punishment would be worse. Once my teacher forced me eat food from the bins in school to teach me to not be 'wasteful'. My mum was away for weeks at a time, travelling and meeting friends. Parenting was difficult for her, as she had my older brother when she was seventeen. She wanted to live like a young girl but had the responsibilities of an adult. She'd drop me and my brothers off at different people's houses. I feared staying at my neighbour's house, as she would violently hit me and leave me without food for the whole day. Her husband had also sexually assaulted me but I said nothing to anyone as I was scared of the consequences. She locked me in a room for almost two days, until my mum came back to collect me. I remember crying, wondering how long I was going to be trapped in the room. When my parents came to pick me up, I smiled and said that the visit was great. Family members and other friends used to speak negative things over my life, saying, 'I wish you would die. Why are you here?' So, I grew up believing that my life was unimportant. I truly believed that if I was to die, no one would care.

My dad was involved in politics at the time, giving orders and fighting in the war against Syria. Our family was threatened because of this, so my dad had to resign. He bought a casino, requiring him to work night shifts and be away for days at a time. At this casino, my dad's friend was talking to him about a man called Jesus. God began softening my dad's heart. He began to reimburse the customers that had lost on betting machines as he felt empathetic towards their situation. My dad was down to his last savings because of this. Moving to England was the safest option because of the political uprising. People were after him and wanted to kill our family, so he spent the last of his savings on trying

ter. The council moved us to a hotel in Hounslow, before transferring us to Leeds months later. From the ages of seven to nine, I went to at least seven primary schools. I became numb, knowing that I couldn't make friends, simply because I would be leaving them. It affected my childhood and the way I communicated with everyone around me. We moved from Leeds to Birmingham and from Birmingham to Luton until we settled in London. Living in Leeds was difficult, as it was not a multicultural place at the time. My mum was pregnant with my younger sister and would have to deal with racial comments. People would throw stones and bricks at our window, telling us to move out of their area, simply because we didn't look like them. I began hiding under my bed again, afraid that someone might knock on the door with a knife.

"Family members and other friends used to speak negative things over my life, saying, "I wish you would die. Why are you here?" So, I grew up believing that my life was unimportant. I truly believed that if I was to die, no one would care."

I was seven years old when I went to a church service in Leeds, months after coming from Lebanon. My dad had been granted a visa

to get us a visa to be able to leave the country. We were so happy when we arrived at the airport, but the embassy rejected our papers. In that moment, my dad prayed for the first time. He got on his knees and said, 'Jesus, let your will be done.' Days later, a friend called my dad and told him that we were able to leave the country as refugees but we had to go as soon as possible. The only condition was that my dad had to wait four months for his own visa before following us to England. We had to leave that night, without suitcases. My mum had a backpack of food. I remember being rushed into the elevator, crying because I wanted to hold my doll one last time.

I came into London as a refugee at the age of seven and was immediately denied a house. We sat on the street, homeless, while my mum tried to contact an old friend. People would walk past and smirk. Some wouldn't even look. My mum contacted an old friend, who offered their house for three days, until we were provided with shel-

and was back with us. He asked me to go to church with him as he didn't want to go alone. I wanted a relationship with the Jesus that the priest was talking about, but I didn't know this Jesus well enough. I grew up in a culture where Jesus was only spoken about when it came to sins. I sat in my bed that night with a card in my hand. I said, 'God, if you're real, please help me pray.' I knew from that moment that I was made for more, that no matter what happened God had good plans for me, plans that involved the younger generation.

I settled into primary school in London at the age of nine. This was the last time we moved. I had a hard time processing things. I remember sitting in the classroom, learning, and I couldn't believe that what I was hearing was real. It was like I was behind glass, unable to break through it. A few weeks ago, I had been in another school, and the year before I had been in a different city; it didn't seem real. I could see the events occurring around me, but I couldn't feel or internalize them. I was bullied by other students and teachers because of this. They'd call me 'dumb' and 'foreign'. I knew I wasn't stupid. I knew that I let the fear of death grip me to the point where I mentally escaped into my thoughts and fantasies, unable to wake up. My English teacher, Mrs Georgio, didn't look down on me because of this but encouraged me to write down my thoughts. She spotted that I had a passion for creative writing before I even knew it myself. She asked to mentor me in English, encouraging me to process my thoughts and turn my dreams into reality. This made primary school easier, although I couldn't make friends with other students. I became angry and impatient with people because I felt misunderstood.

This made transitioning into secondary school difficult. I was excluded several times for fighting. My fears began to change. I didn't fear death anymore; I feared living. It was like a self-fulfilling prophecy. I became the person the world wanted me to become. I was a bully, not letting anyone speak to me in a way I did not like. All of this was done out of fear. I'd wake up with anxiety and sleep

with the same anxiety lingering in the pit of my stomach. I didn't want to live anymore.

The culture I had grown up with was so gang-related. The guys I spoke to in school were selling drugs, bribing the boys in the younger years to work for them. Because I grew up with these people, their wrongdoings were okay in my eyes because they were like family to me. The more you become familiar with someone, the harder it is for you to see in hindsight the damage that they are causing you. I didn't see the damage it was causing them or me. I'd spend my days hanging out with boys, while they'd sell cocaine and other drugs. I'd hold money for them, not caring about the consequences because I no longer feared dying. I just didn't want to live.

I remember almost believing that was all God had for me. The memories of the seven-year-old girl asking God to be in control of her life in Leeds were fading. But another voice in my head was whispering, 'What are you doing here?' I'd go home and ignore that voice every night because I hated myself. I used to hit myself because I thought that that's what I deserved. I thought that aggression and discipline would drive out anxiety and fear. The hitting didn't work, so I'd cut myself, hoping that the bleeding could release my pain, not fully understanding that my pain was solely internal.

I hated the way I looked because I was told that my eyebrows were too thick and that my nose was too long. I thought that the only way to be happy was to mould myself into who people wanted me to be. I started seeking affirmation from different males. Every few weeks I would like a new guy, until I realized that he could not fulfil me. Then I'd move on to the next one. The depression and anxiety that I went through in secondary school was the hardest struggle, because it felt like someone was holding a mirror in front of me, forcing me to see my brokenness and face my fears. I didn't want to face the fact that I hated and blamed my mum for the way I was. It strained our relationship because we had never shared a conversation about anything important. I didn't think it was normal for a young girl to have a relationship with her mother until I saw other girls speaking to their mums and hugging them.

From the age of sixteen, I'd sit in the Catholic church at the top of my road almost every day at seven o'clock. I didn't actually know what I was doing there, but I knew that I was searching for something. I'd ask God to provide a way out for me but I'd wake up the next morning and seek affirmation from the same people. I knew I needed a miracle because the culture that I was in was intoxicating. I'd go out with my friends every Friday and Saturday. People at parties would come up to me and my friends and pull out guns, asking us if we knew a certain person from a certain area. I didn't care because I was desperate for a family. The older drug dealers would speak life over us, which was ironic. They would say things that our family members didn't say, such as, 'You've got potential. You're going to change the world.' Because of this, I saw young boys turn into young men. I saw young girls (including myself) mould themselves into whoever these young men wanted them to be. The people I grew up with were innocent. They, too, were searching, but they found the wrong thing – actually, they were found by the wrong thing. Their loyalty and consistency, if channelled into the right thing, could have changed the world. I saw an innocent child who was being bullied and wanted to be protected. I saw a child whose single mum couldn't pay the bills and a child whose parents were refugees and so I did not want to detach myself from the culture because I was the culture. By the age of seventeen, I was fighting girls who were showing up at my doorstep and receiving and reciprocating death threats. I thought that if the world made me aggressive, I was going to be the best aggressive person the world's ever seen!

A few months later, my best friend Neyla asked me to come to a 'celebration' at a warehouse with her and my other friend Elijah. I thought, why not? We were all going for the first time, so we didn't know what to expect. On our way to this place, we got lost and I remember impatiently telling Neyla, 'I'm never coming here again!' Little did I know that my life was about to be very different. I walked into a warehouse and saw hundreds of young people with their hands raised, worshipping God. I genuinely didn't know that so many young people who loved Jesus could exist. I saw the emotion on their face and was taken aback. I thought, 'Wow, God, you've wanted me to be here since the day I was born. You planned everything so that I would come here at the age of seventeen. You died so that I can have this moment.' I thought that 'church' consisted of me sitting at the top of my road and crying to God by myself

> "I didn't care because I was desperate for a family. The older drug dealers would speak life over us, which was ironic. They would say things that our family members didn't say, such as 'You've got potential. You're going to change the world.'"

in a building. But these young people, they were the church. I knew that something in me shifted that day. I didn't realize this at the time, but I immediately began distancing myself from the toxic culture I was raised in. On a Friday evening, I'd go and hang with people who spoke life over me, rather than going to another house party. I began to understand the toxicity of the culture I was in and that death was never the answer. These young people that I met at the church would tell me that they loved me and that I was a light in the world. Everything made sense. Last year, when I was praying alone in the church at the top of my road, I was actually praying for this and I didn't even know it!

I moved to Southampton to study English at university at the age of eighteen and was overjoyed. I couldn't believe that God had brought me this far! The first year of university was very hard because I was distant from the new people I had met at Hillsong and I was not talking to my family. I realized that I still had a lot of built-up depression and bitterness in me. The day I tried to commit suicide was the day I surrendered my life to Christ. I thought that it would come in the form of me raising my hand in a church service, but God needed me to come to the end of myself, to wholeheartedly place my life in his hands. I sat in my dorm room, cutting myself deeply. I was about to cut into my veins, when I heard a voice say, 'What are you doing?' In that moment, I felt an overwhelming peace surround me, a peace that assured me that God had good plans for me. I opened my Bible and began to read Hebrews 12:1. It went: 'For the Lord disciplines the one

leader. I was amazed, because I didn't know that youth leaders existed! I remember always telling my friends that my future will include God and youth but I didn't know how to mould the two together. I said yes and kept travelling down every week for three years, leading a gathering every Friday evening and calling the youth during the week. Leading these youth changed my life. I began to love myself even more through showing just how much they are loved. Sowing into them impacted my life more than theirs! I was writing at the time, and I had it on my heart to perform a poem for Young and Free Conference in 2016. I was prompted to write it, in faith, not knowing the outcome. I waited and prepared in the shadows. A few weeks after, my friend Kwaku, a rapper, messaged me and asked me to help him write a spoken word poem to perform for Conference. I was blown away! Because of this, I now get to lead young writers. God turns all things around because if I hadn't had so much aggression and anger built up inside me, I would have never picked up a paper and a pen. Everything I've been through has allowed me to serve God wholeheartedly.

> "The day I tried to commit suicide was the day I surrendered my life to Christ. I thought that it would come in the form of me raising my hand in a church service, but God needed me to come to the end of myself, to wholeheartedly place my life in his hands."

he loves.' That was the last time I self-harmed because I realized that cutting myself wasn't God's discipline; it was me trying to discipline myself over burdens that I should have given to God. The real discipline was restraining from self-harm. I began to understand that God's discipline is not like the discipline I received as a child. It was a sound discipline. It was a whisper – a nudge towards a narrow road that my friends in school did not walk down. God's discipline over my life was not comfortable but I knew that it was not to kill me or belittle me. It was to ultimately give me life. From that moment, the joy of living began to overpower the fear that I had of death. I remembered the encounter I had when I was seven. It was as if God whispered into my heart that I was going to do something for his kingdom all along. I felt prompted to travel from London to Southampton weekly ever since.

A few months after coming along to church, Elijah came to me and asked me to be a youth

around because if I hadn't had so much aggression and anger built up inside me, I would have never picked up a paper and a pen. Everything I've been through has allowed me to serve God wholeheartedly.

Currently, the goal is to complete a master's in Creative Writing and Literature while continuing to sow into the youth in the ministry. The long term plan is to write novels and get young people off the street, through facilitating them with a Poetry Café, where they're able to sit and write together, with mentors who speak life over them and encourage them positively. Rap culture and poetry was a big thing in my generation and it still is. If my friends and I had a place to go to 'spit' (another word for rap and write), we would have been able to create healthy narratives for our lives, rather than letting our lives be influenced by negative role models. My story shows God can do more than we can ever imagine if we cast our fears on him.

Sweat—drops linger beneath the plastic.
This mask, glued with fear,
has become my home.
No one can see through these eyes
even though I'm wearing a see—through disguise.

Often, I feel knocking on my face,
the sound of a doorbell ringing in my ear
but I close these curtains
hoping that they'd believe that nobody is home.
I thicken the foundation on my cheek,
hoping they'd mistake it for my flesh.

The need for affirmation is addictive
It's an unusual drug,
one that does not need to be swallowed.
It runs through these veins like crushed
antibiotics in water;
I wave goodbye to the reflection
in the mirror every morning.
— Carine Harb

ERWIN RAPHAEL McMANUS

"Fear is the battle line to the next great
breakthrough in your life."

FEAR OF DEATH

> **"** I just made it my practice in life that when I was afraid of something I leaned in and did it because I realized that fear is like a phantom. If you bring light to it, it disappears. **"**

Starting at the beginning of your story, do you see ways your parents helped guide you in overcoming fear or becoming resilient in your life during your childhood? I never knew my father so he didn't play a part in that – other than genetics, ha! My mom left me with my grandparents until I was five, so during those very early years both of my parents were largely absent. In a way those decisions and how they impacted me probably made me very resilient. For me, resilience isn't necessarily developed by people doing right in your life; it's developed by how you respond to whatever happens in your life – good and bad.

In *Fearfully Made* **we are exploring the big five fears many of us have to face and overcome: failure, ridicule, rejection, loneliness and death. Growing up, did you struggle with these. If so, do any in particular stand out?** My biggest fear in my life growing up and even in adulthood is the fear of not accomplishing anything great. Whatever one of those categories that falls into!

Well, it could fall into most, but maybe failure would be the most appropriate? No, I am not afraid of failure. I am really comfortable with failure because I've known it all my life. I do not fear loneliness because I have known loneliness. I think you fear things that you are unfamiliar with. We try to run from our fears, but the best way to overcome your fears is to

"ear of God is the only fear that establishes freedom, because perfect love casts away fear, and so there is no room for fear in love.**"**

become comfortable with them. I just made it my practice in life that when I was afraid of something I leaned in and did it because I realized that fear is like a phantom. If you bring light to it, it disappears. But I still think there's an overwhelming fear that I will never accomplish that one beautiful thing that I was created to do. And that does haunt me.

What do you think is most important for people to understand about prayer in overcoming fear? The Bible tells us there is no fear in love, and that God himself is love, so spending time with God through prayer naturally expels fear. Whatever you fear establishes the boundaries of your freedom. If you fear heights, you stay low; if you fear people, you stay alone. Your fear establishes the boundaries, and so your fear becomes your master. Fear of God is the only fear that establishes freedom, because perfect love casts away fear, and so there is no room for fear in love.

The Bible tells us that God works all things for our good. In light of that, how do you think God uses fear to teach us to fight? I see fear as a lot like pain. I really almost never take any medication because pain makes you understand where the healing has to take place. If you dull the pain, you don't know how to focus the healing. To me fear is the same. It's the pain of the soul telling you where your freedom is. If you dull the fear, and you don't lean into it, you won't

be able to find your freedom. Fear is the battle line to the next great breakthrough in your life.

The word 'phobia' literally means fear, so when we live with phobias, we live with fear. Too often we can turn our phobias into diseases, with the solution being medication, not transformation. Many people self-medicate fears with security and safety, comfort, steady income, predictability, by being in relationships we shouldn't be in. We self-medicate ourselves by removing risk and uncertainty and the unknown from our lives. And for me that is the way that we dull the pain of a life not well lived. I'd rather feel the fear, lean into it and see transformation.

Do you think that there are any misconceptions about fear that some Christians may be operating under? That fear makes you a coward. It does not: it makes you human. If there were no fear, there would be no courage. We have this view that there are courageous people and there are fearful people, but there are really just fearful people – some who choose courage and others who choose retreat. I think it's interesting that in Joshua 1, God says, 'Fear not, fear not, fear not. Be courageous, be courageous, be courageous.' That's how you know that Joshua is scared to death, because God wouldn't have said that over and over again if Joshua had not been afraid.

If I look back at my own life, I think it's funny because people have often said I am courageous about the times

" Fear doesn't diminish you. It's your response to fear that diminishes you, so don't be afraid of fear. "

I was most fearful. I felt fear. I just didn't want my fear to define me. Other times, I am so set on what God has for that moment that I just forget to be fearful. I've had times where I'd be in the middle of massive drug cartels, with machine guns everywhere, cocaine stacked up to the roof, and I'd walk into them, talk about Jesus and come out alive. People would ask, 'Were you afraid?' And I look back and realize I just forgot to be! I think we get paralyzed in fear because we are not actively moving forward in life. So we need to move forward with concentrating on living a highly intentional life, and whatever comes, comes.

What advice would you offer a Christian that feels a sense of guilt about feeling fearful because they want to have faith in every situation? Fear isn't the absence of faith. If there is a lion in the room and it's hungry and you're the only one there, are you saying you shouldn't be afraid? Some people just aren't afraid because they're just too stupid to understand how dangerous one is. Fear doesn't diminish you. It's your response to fear that diminishes you, so don't be afraid of fear.

For those that don't know, you're a cancer survivor. When the doctors told you that you had cancer, what did you feel and think and fear? When I got told the news, I gave myself permission to feel whatever I wanted to feel. I told myself,

if I get afraid, I'm okay with that. If I get super-angry, I'm okay with that. Regardless of being a Christian or a pastor, I didn't feel the need to feel all the right things.

At the same time, I didn't let other people force me to feel things either. You know, if someone came into the room feeling sad, I understood but I also wouldn't let their inability to handle the moment be my monitor. I'm sorry but you do not get to have cancer for me. So when I didn't feel any fear, bitterness or anger, I was kind of shocked! I kept waiting for that onrush of negative emotion, but none of it came. And I didn't have a struggle with faith, but I was okay if I did. I gave myself permission to get mad at or question God. It's only part of being human. In the end, I just kept thinking, 'Wow, Jesus is everything he said he would be.'

In fact my daughter got mad at me because I said to God that I was willing to go through everything that would allow me to have a greater voice in people's lives. My daughter said to me, 'Are you out of your mind? Why would you pray that?' She was mad because she wanted me to live. That was the hardest thing – my family's reactions.

I have to say this: what I didn't expect is how many people with cancer would come up and talk to me. How many people there were who were really hurting. If my cancer can help me empathize or give someone faith or encourage them to overcome, then I'm sure God will have used it for good.

 ERWIN RAPHAEL McMANUS is an artist, entrepreneur, cultural-thought leader and the founder of MOSAIC, a church in Los Angeles, California and has inspired the church across the world to new expressions of faith and spirituality. MOSAIC is known for its innovation, creativity, diversity, and social entrepreneurism and has been named one of the most influential and innovative churches in America. His travels have taken him to over 50 countries and he has spoken to over a million people from a wide variety of audiences, including professional athletes, Wall Street investors, universities, film studios, and conferences focused on leadership, creativity, culture, and living a holistic life. Visit him online at www.erwinmcmanus.com.

THE LORD IS
MY LIGHT AND
MY SALVATION;
WHOM SHALL I FEAR?
THE LORD IS
THE STRONGHOLD
OF MY LIFE;
OF WHOM SHALL
I BE AFRAID?

PSALM 27:1 (ESV)

GROUP DISCUSSION ✕ QUESTIONS
CHAPTER 5 FEAR OF DEATH

Growing up in war-torn Beirut, Carine seemed to be surrounded by death. In a country that has been almost consistently embroiled in both internal and external conflict since the 1970s, and where hundreds of thousands have lost their lives, it's not surprising that so many in her community become almost blasé about the ongoing loss of life around them. But are we blasé because we have settled the issue of death, or blasé from self-protection – a desperate attempt to distance ourselves from the reality that death is indeed coming for every single one of us?

A pastor reflecting on the difficulties of death at the funeral of an elderly man asked the congregation a similar question: 'Why, if death is guaranteed for all of us, have we still not truly come to terms with it?' After a thoughtful pause, he continued, 'Perhaps it was because we were never designed to come to terms with it. If we take a fish out of water and hope that it breathes, we are only fooling ourselves. A fish was never designed to breathe in the open air. If we present a human with death and tell them to be okay with it, we too are fools, for a human was never designed to deal with the end of a life.'

The fear of death (also known as thanatophobia) is multidimensional. It can focus on the actual process of dying and the physical harm and pain that precedes the moment of death. It can stem from intense guilt and remorse that comes from not being able to stop the death of a loved one. The greatest fear of death, however, is existential: the fear arising from the fact that none of us confidently knows what happens to our existence once death arrives.

Yes, the Bible affirms that those who are in Christ will be with him in a place of peace and

eternal joy, but the details can be unclear. Despite this promise, we can still be filled with difficult emotions: dread over the uncertainty and finality; regret that accompanies unfinished plans or unspoken words; the pain of being separated from the future lives of our loved ones; and the fear of possible judgment, retribution and punishment when faced with our Creator, to name but a few.

Death is real. Yet, as Elizabeth reminds us, it did not take God by surprise. He is the Creator and Author of life, the One who defeated death, and the One who promises to carry us safely through to the other side.

REFLECTION QUESTIONS

1. Why do we fear death?

2. In your own personal contemplation, what is the most disturbing aspect of death and dying?

3. The fears of failure, ridicule, rejection and loneliness come together powerfully at the thought of death. What will happen when we in our fragility and brokenness are finally confronted by a holy God? Read 1 Corinthians 1:4-9, focusing on verses 8-9. How will we be seen in the Day of the Lord Jesus Christ? Whose faithfulness will ensure this? How does that impact our fear of facing God at the time of death?

4. Those in Christ will stand before God without fear of rejection or condemnation. The Bible is clear on this. Yet we still will face a type of judgement. Read 2 Corinthians 5:10. What will be the purpose of this judgement? How does knowledge affect how we go about our daily living on earth?

5. Read Revelation 21:1-4. How does John describe the atmosphere of heaven? How can this help us overcome the fear of death?

6. In heaven, we will finally be in the presence of the full, unrestrained and perfect love of God. Read 1 John 4:18. What will the perfect love of God do for each person in his presence? Imagine your life with all of your fears driven out. Now, imagine the lives of your family and friends with all of their fears driven out. What would life look like for this group of people? Finally, imagine that happening for billions upon billions of people for all of eternity. What does life in heaven look like now?

CHAPTER 6 FEAR OF GOD

"FOR AS HIGH AS THE HEAVENS ARE ABOVE THE EARTH, SO GREAT IS HIS STEADFAST LOVE TOWARDS THOSE WHO FEAR HIM; AS FAR AS THE EAST IS FROM THE WEST, SO FAR DOES HE REMOVE OUR TRANSGRESSIONS FROM US." PSALM 103:11-12 (ESV)

FEAR OF GOD

STAND IN AWE

BY: DAN WATSON

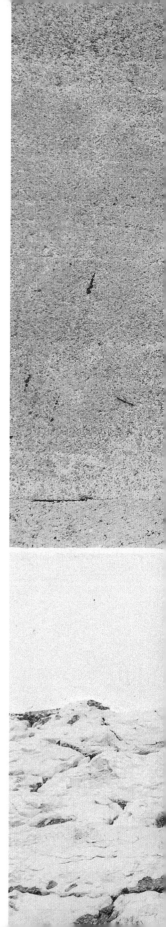

As youth and young adults today, it can seem like we're surrounded by fears – and it doesn't take a genius to see that many of these pressures are social ones: fitting in, being liked, being as popular or cool as everyone else. We come to see ourselves the way the world sees us. We spend so much time focusing on what's on the outside that we forget to cultivate what's on the inside. And yet the Bible tells us that perfect love drives out fear. Clearly, God wants us to live like we are made for more.

Made to Shape Society

Far from what society tries to tells us, the Bible is clear: it's really all about what's inside you. Matthew 12:35 says, 'The good person out of his good treasure brings forth good, and the evil person out of his evil treasure brings forth evil.' My mum always used to say, 'Garbage in, garbage out.' Basically, what is in you will come out!

God reminds us of this again and again through the characters of the Bible, characters like Daniel. Daniel 6 says, 'Now Daniel so distinguished himself among the administrators and the governors by his exceptional qualities that the king planned to set him over the whole kingdom.' Daniel focused as much on his gifts as on his character. But Daniel had haters. He got put in his position because of who he was, and administrators tried to find grounds for charges against him, but they could find no corruption in him. Even the haters knew he was made for so much more.

We don't have to fearfully fit into the culture that exists. We are called to bring the culture the Jesus way: a fearless kingdom culture that positively shapes society.

Fear of God

If love drives out fear, why does the Bible say we are to fear God? 'Fearing' God in this context doesn't mean being afraid. It means living in awe of God and setting our minds on him instead of worrying about what the world thinks. Society tells us to fear others. The Bible tells us to fear God alone! In Matthew 10:22, Jesus says, 'You will be hated because of me, but the one who stands firm will be saved.' Standing firm sometimes means stepping out – stepping out of people's opinions and voices in our lives and stepping into the presence of the God, setting our minds on him.

In Colossians 3:2, when Paul is in prison, he tells us, 'Set your mind on the things above, not on earthly things.' If we're going to be a people who shape society, then

"IF LOVE DRIVES OUT FEAR, WHY DOES THE BIBLE SAY WE ARE TO FEAR GOD? 'FEARING' GOD IN THIS CONTEXT DOESN'T MEAN BEING AFRAID. IT MEANS LIVING IN AWE OF GOD AND SETTING OUR MINDS ON HIM INSTEAD OF WORRYING ABOUT WHAT THE WORLD THINKS."

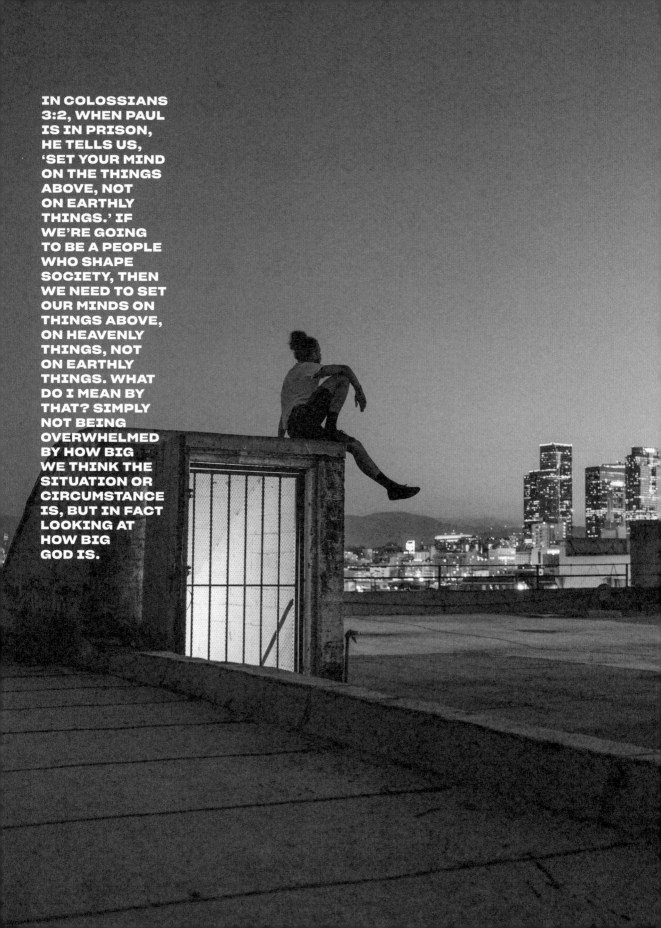

IN COLOSSIANS 3:2, WHEN PAUL IS IN PRISON, HE TELLS US, 'SET YOUR MIND ON THE THINGS ABOVE, NOT ON EARTHLY THINGS.' IF WE'RE GOING TO BE A PEOPLE WHO SHAPE SOCIETY, THEN WE NEED TO SET OUR MINDS ON THINGS ABOVE, ON HEAVENLY THINGS, NOT ON EARTHLY THINGS. WHAT DO I MEAN BY THAT? SIMPLY NOT BEING OVERWHELMED BY HOW BIG WE THINK THE SITUATION OR CIRCUMSTANCE IS, BUT IN FACT LOOKING AT HOW BIG GOD IS.

we need to set our minds on things above, on heavenly things, not on earthly things. What do I mean by that? Simply not being overwhelmed by how big we think the situation or circumstance is, but in fact looking at how big God is. It's all about getting the right perspective. The only way we can be delivered from fear of this world is by fearing God, which is why we need to learn to set our minds on him.

At seventeen years old I found myself in a police cell, and for a moment in my life I believed what society said about me. Because of some of my upbringing, the world would class me as just another statistic. And in that cell I remember saying, 'God, if you're real, then I'm going to make a decision right now. I'm not going to believe what society says about me anymore. I'm going to set my mind… I'm going to set my mind on heavenly things, not on earthly things.'

Even then the enemy wanted to take my mind, saying, 'What do you have except for a broken background and now a criminal record? How could you do great things for God, Dan?' And I started thinking: Noah did amazing things because he had an ark; David killed a giant with a stone. Then I realized this: I have the most powerful thing in the world that holds more weight and authority than anything else. We have a name that is above every other name. We can do all things. We are called and we are chosen because of the name of Jesus.

You see, my life may have looked like it was going in one direction, but I turned away from fear towards the only one to be truly 'feared'. Statistically, I should not be here but in setting our minds on God we don't have to be the statistic. We can change the narrative.

The Right Perspective

The Bible shows us how we can see the world through God's eyes instead of the world's eyes. In John 4, Jesus has a conversation with a Samaritan woman. She tries to put up hurdles or barriers to protect herself, thinking, 'You don't care enough that you're going to jump this barrier I'm putting up.' One of the barriers she puts up is culture: 'We're so different. In our traditions we don't talk to each other. Jew and Samaritan don't interact with each other. You're from a different culture.' But you know that culture is man-made. The thing that I love about God and his people is that we were all made in the image of Christ, so he does not see us for our colour or our gender. He sees us for who we are. We are called, we're accepted, we're forgiven, we're victorious, we're free and we're children of God. That's how he sees us.

Instead of arguing with the woman, Jesus shares the truth with her. He can see that she's so caught up by thinking the way the world thinks. But he sparks a conversation with her because he has a goal in mind: to see that woman in a relationship with God.

She tells him that she has no husband, and Jesus replies, 'The fact is, you have had five husbands, and the man you now have is not your husband.' He calls her out on the things that make society say, 'You're not good, you can't, you won't, you never will.' He calls her out on the things that she thinks separate her from anything great in her life. But here's what I love about God. He's not calling her out to condemn her. He's calling her out to show her that not even her sin can stop him from loving her. This is what happens when we see each other through God's eyes rather than through the eyes of this world. We become transformed and we can live not in fear of society, but in awe of God.

Live Your Best Life

Jesus tells this Samaritan woman, 'Whoever drinks the water I give them will never thirst. Indeed, the water I give them will become in them a spring of water welling up to eternal life.' Jesus has greater things for the women than she could ever imagine or expect.

No matter what you're searching for or trying to find, Jesus can and will exceed it. David, in Psalm 27:4, decides to set his mind on God: 'One thing have I desired of the Lord, that will I seek after; that I may dwell in the house of the Lord all the days of my life, to behold the beauty of the Lord, and to enquire in his temple.'

I wonder today what your want is. What's the desire of your heart? If we're going to live the Jesus way and shape society, our desire must be all about Jesus, to know him more, to get into his presence.

There's so much I want in life. But more than anything I want to follow Jesus, to know Jesus. For David wanted 'one thing'. You can be distracted by all these other things, or you can be attracted to the ways of God. Think about the best thing possible for your life. Whatever it is, God has greater for you. John 10:10 says Jesus came to give you life to the full. He truly wants you to live your best life.

DAN WATSON is the Youth & Young Adult Pastor of Hillsong Church UK, overseeing the church's Youth Ministry. He is married to Joanne and they have two amazing children, Isabella East and Jude Jenson. Born and raised in the East End of London, Dan did not have the easiest of childhoods but decided to change the narrative of what society says about him and others. He is passionate about positively shaping society by pointing people to Jesus so that they can live out their best lives.

Since the children are made of flesh and blood, it's logical that the Savior took on flesh and blood in order to rescue them by his death. By embracing death, taking it into himself, he destroyed the Devil's hold on death and freed all who cower through life, scared to death of death. It's obvious, of course, that he didn't go to all this trouble for angels. It was for people like us, the children of Abraham. That's why he had to enter into every detail of human life. Then, when he came before God as high priest to get rid of the people's sins, he would have already experienced it all himself – all the pain, all the testing – and would be able to help where help was needed.

HEBREWS 2:14-18 (MSG)

RODRIGUE
VUNDILU

POSITIVELY SHAPING SOCIETY X PARIS

HILLSONG YOUTH X YOUNG ADULTS

Where were you born? I was born in Kinshasa in Congo and now live in Paris, France.

What do you do? I'm currently working in a hotel as a receptionist

What hobbies do you have? I love rapping, acting and doing sport. I also love reading poetry!

Who inspires you to be fearless and why? It might sound a cliché but I'd definitely say Jesus. Not just because I am a Christian but because, after reading his story in the Bible, anyone can see that the man was fearless and has inspired generations.

What were you scared of as a child? Also cliché, but I was scared of the dark!

What's the biggest risk you've taken? Talking to a girl! I'm a bit shy when it comes to expressing my feelings.

Are there any key Bible verses you live by to overcome fear? It's a famous one: Isaiah 41:10. 'So do not fear, for I am with you; do not be dismayed, for I am your God. I will strengthen you and help you; I will uphold you with my righteous right hand.'

Do you have a favourite book that's helped you on your spiritual journey? No, but I am looking forward to reading Joyce Meyers' book *Battlefield of the Mind*.

"DON'T BE AFRAID BECAUSE, IF GOD PUT IT IN YOUR HEART, YOU'D BETTER BELIEVE IT. EARTH IS THE PLACE TO FOLLOW YOUR DREAM AND MAKE IT HAPPEN. YOU BELIEVE IN GOD, YOU LOVE GOD AND YOU HAVE A GIFT FROM GOD. SO WHY ARE YOU AFRAID TO OPEN THE GIFT FROM SOMEONE YOU LOVE?"

What do you think about hope in today's culture that tells us to put our hope in things like fame, fortune and success?
I definitely think we hope for the wrong thing in society today. Fame, fortune and success won't be remembered, but the way we treat and love people will have a lasting impact. Fame and success are just titles the world gives you, but love is what we can give the world! Instead of hoping for these things, we should hope for people to read Matthew 22:39 and the commandment to love your neighbour and apply it in our everyday lives.

How has your relationship with Jesus redefined how you view and overcome fear? Because I know with Jesus I have already won, every time I'm facing fear I just think about him and all he went through for me. I also know that anything I'll face can't be worse than

what Jesus faced while he was on earth. He is like my hero so I want to be as fearless as him.

Fear of God means that we stand in awe, in wonder of him. What do you think is powerful and important about remembering the greatness and goodness of God? The fact of being sure about it! You only need to experience his greatness once to remember that he will always be there for you, and that's what I think is so powerful! We don't even deserve it.

Where do you feel God is leading you in the future? Right now I am on an internship where I can clearly see that God is using me for a purpose for his kingdom. In my heart I feel like he is leading me to lead a massive group of young people to him with what I do best, which is music… just spreading his word and

maybe one day starting my own church.

What advice would you give the next generation, wanting to follow a dream but feeling fearful? Don't be afraid because, if God put it in your heart, you'd better believe it. Earth is the place to follow your dream and make it happen. You believe in God, you love God and you have a gift from God. So why are you afraid to open the gift from someone you love? The only way to find out if you can be who you want to be is to try.

What does 'fear of God' mean to you? It's like when a son fears his father, not because he is going to punish him but because his father is wiser and smarter. That's how I feel about God. He is in control. To fear God is like a protection because I know if God provides boundaries it is only because he loves us.

Can you recall a specific time in your life where you have seen God's love and faith overcome fear? In my family. Our situation completely shifted from bad to good. I was afraid that my relationship with my parents would never be like normal families. As a kid I didn't live with my parents, so when I finally joined them in Europe I didn't want to feel like they were my parents, although in my heart I knew they were. Throughout my adolescence I always disrespected them and we often fought. I always thought they didn't love me and that the situation would never get better.

Many years later I started going to church, at first just because the people were really nice. But my life really changed when I got baptized, because that's the night when I really felt the presence of God and also the fear of God but in a positive way. From that

"NOW THIS LIFESTYLE JUST FEELS NORMAL FOR ME. I SEE LIFE AS JOURNEY THAT WE DON'T HAVE THE 'LIMIT' DATE FOR. SO I LEARNT TO LIVE EVERY DAY LIKE IT'S THE LAST AND APPRECIATED WHAT GOD PROVIDES AND THE OPPORTUNITIES HE OFFERS ME MORE."

point on I have experienced his love for me and my family. He made me wiser and more mature, and now my parents are like my best friends.

Tell us about the night of 13 November 2015. What happened from lying on your bed to seeing people on Facebook telling you to stay at home? How did you feel? What kind of fear did you feel? The night of the terrorist attacks I was in my room with my cousin who had come to spend the week with me. I was on Facebook and as I was scrolling down I saw someone post about the terrorist attacks. I noticed they weren't far from my home so I went into the living room with my cousin and we turned on the TV to watch the news. We could even hear the police cars outside the window. As it got worse, we went to check that the whole family was at home. Thankfully, they were.

I realized in that moment how important my family were to me. There wasn't a lot we could do so we went to sleep, but the next morning as I went to work there was just this atmosphere of fear in the air.

What did the attacks teach you about where you put your security? That we can be disappointed by putting our security in people because we don't know what to expect. But with God you know that: 'Your security is your faith in him.'

What were the streets of Paris like after? Did you think you were going to have your youth gathering that night? Can you describe the atmosphere in the room? That night the streets were very quiet. People were afraid to go out, and none of us thought we'd still have the youth gathering, but our pastors confirmed it.

There were more people than we thought there'd be. It was one of the most powerful youth services we have ever had. A generation gathered together declaring, 'We will not be shaken,' over ourselves and over our city. Just an overwhelming sense of peace and that everything was going to be okay.

What is the power of praise and worship, singing of God's goodness in the face of fear? I can now say that it makes us feel fearless and we know that nothing and no one is more powerful than God, because when you give yourself away to him nothing else matters – nothing at all.

Tell us about prayer in connecting with God, especially in times that can be fearful? I like to hear God tell me that he is still in control, especially after a fearful situation like the attacks. When he does,

he takes my eyes off the horrible situation and puts them on him. He gives me the courage to go out, to keep loving people, to keep believing.

So for me praying is definitely the key to getting through fear.

Do you think you live your life differently now than before the attacks – in how you see life, in what you say yes to doing? In the weeks after the attack, I lived my life differently. I loved deeper, laughed more and louder, prayed more. Now this lifestyle just feels normal for me.

I see life as journey that we don't have the 'limit' date for. So I learnt to live every day like it's the last and appreciated what God provides and the opportunities he offers me more. I am less scared about saying what is in my mind and heart and of talking more about Jesus with people.

THE LIGHT SHINES IN THE DARKNESS AND THE DARKNESS HAS NOT OVERCOME IT.

JOHN 1:5 (NIV)

WILLIAM ADOASI

"They don't have a male to look up to, so they search for identity from those around them. They're looking to older guys. I'm the firstborn of seven children and so I always wanted an older brother to come and defend me. I could definitely see how, if I had stayed in that environment and wasn't protected from it, I would look to the older people for guidance and for a kind of identity."

" TELL US ABOUT GROWING UP IN A FAMILY WITH SIX SIBLINGS. WHERE DID YOU GROW UP?

I grew up on a council estate in Camberwell. For the first thirteen years of my life, nine of us were sharing a two-bedroomed house. So I haven't come from ideal circumstances. My parents are from Ghana, with my dad growing up in a remote village where he didn't even have the basics for school. He sometimes went barefoot. In the area I grew up in I've got friends who are in jail for life for various different things and some who are sadly no longer here.

How were the dynamics of family life growing up? Growing up in a family of nine, we all chipped in any way we could. My mum would be there for us in the daytime and worked night shifts. My dad's the head pastor of a church, which now has eight branches worldwide, but at the time it was just one struggling church in south London. So my mum did all she could to help support his vision. My dad just worked his butt off for the kingdom to push things forward, so was a great example growing up.

How did they protect you as you were growing up? I felt super-shielded from the world and, at the time, I didn't get it and it used to upset me – like curfews were ridiculous! My parents have a ridiculously good discerning spirit. So there were people I was really good friends with that they would basically say I couldn't be friends with anymore. At the time, they were totally on the straight and narrow.

I look back now and see some of those people's lives and where they've ended up, and it's just crazy how my parents could see that before. My dad sent me to after-school tutoring, so I used to be there most evenings. Through that tutoring and him pushing me, they ended up sending me to boarding school near Birmingham from eleven to sixteen, which obviously further shielded me.

How did you feel those first few nights in boarding school with all these new people? It was quite exciting. It was like, 'I'm away from home. I'm independent now. I'm a big boy.' The first few days you get around. You start playing sport with everyone. I was really into my sports growing up, so I was really loving it at first. It was good.

Did you feel like you had to grow up quite quickly? Yeah, I definitely think I did. You stand on your own two feet – well, kind of – from a really young age. I was interacting with people from all walks of life. And at times you do feel very alone and isolated. I only got into the school through bursaries and scholarships, and sometimes I would hear the people in school that had just got in because their parents could afford it referring to the locals as 'council estate scum'. They didn't know that I live just like those people. So it brought the harsh realities of life to me from a young age.

Did you have any significant fears at that age? Was there a fear of rejection because of where you'd come from? One hundred percent. I remember trying to do anything I could to fit in. When I was younger, I was extremely short. I only started growing when I was about sixteen. So I had so many different insecurities and so many fears, I would literally do anything. I ended up being the loud, funny guy, messing around in class so that people would laugh, just craving attention.

Can you see the same need to fit in amongst the people you grew up with? Yeah. I think that for a lot of young people – especially the young people that I grew up with – they didn't have dads growing up or they came from broken homes. A lot of them, I feel, are searching for identity. They don't have a male to look up to, so they search for identity from those around them. They're looking to older guys. I'm the firstborn of seven children and so I always wanted an older brother to come and defend me. I could definitely see how, if I had stayed in that environment and wasn't protected from it, I would look to the older people for guidance and for a kind of identity. The outworking of that is them getting you to do things that just aren't right.

Was there an element of fear around this hierarchy and these people? Were there any gangs? Massively. I grew up in Camberwell, which at the time they called No Man's Land because it was in between Peckham and Brixton, the rival gangs at the time. It was a pretty dangerous area. The worst time to live in my area was around fireworks season, because people would have firework wars all the time. They would literally just be hitting fireworks at each other. I was mugged once too, when I was sixteen. I had the knife poked into my leg and my throat. And that was when I was in Brixton. You're always aware of it, and that changed my life. I was always on edge, always looking out.

Do you think that's had any impact on your drive now and what you're doing today? Yes, definitely. I don't ever want my future kids to have to go through what I went through. I think it's the same with my dad. He's worked hard to bring us here. Even though I say the area where I grew up was bad, it's nowhere near as bad as where he's come from. So I'm really grateful for what I have. And my whole dream is to take the level up for my children in the next generation. So I think it's been a massive driver for me.

And one of my biggest passions is, especially for young black boys from the area I grew up in, giving them an example of a difference. All they're told about is the negative and the bad examples, and that's all they see around them. And I just want to show them that, hey, look, we've come from the exact same area, same background, but you can turn your life around. You can be better. You don't have to play to the stereotypes.

Growing up with a dad who's a pastor, what led you to the Lord? I wouldn't say I had a definitive moment. I probably put my hand up at every altar call we did at every different youth event, so you could say when I was really young. But did I know God for myself back then? I'd probably say no. It's

just been a process for me. But it's crazy because I've always been passionate about the things of Church and the things of God. When I was in Years 8 and 9, even at my boarding school, I'd run Bible study and try to get people to come. But then, ages sixteen and seventeen, I was doing things that I shouldn't, so I don't know if there was a definitive time. But I've always believed that there's a God, and to me Jesus is the only solution. Jesus is the only thing that could ever work and could ever make sense.

Do any other fears stand out growing up that you feel God's helped you overcome? Failure's one for me. I think because of trying to be accepted and trying to be seen as good. I reckon it's something I still deal with from time to time. Like, you don't want to ever be seen as failing. And because you don't want to fail, you live a safe life and do things that everyone else is doing. You follow the 'normal' path. I was really passionate about sport and if you mess up doing anything sporty, it's there for anyone to see.

Now it's the social media age. There is always that fear that you will be perceived in a bad light. It's scary to think that I was living my life based on how people saw me and felt about me. So that's definitely one thing I've overcome, and I'm overcoming. I guess that ties in with loneliness as well: scared of being the outcast. So you live a life which isn't the unique way God wants you to live your life, because you're trying to fit in with everyone.

When you step out to do something that's significant, you can often feel there is an attack on your thinking, which gets caught up in what you think others might say or think about you. Do you feel like that sometimes? One hundred percent. I know we're not always great at mentioning him, but the devil does not want us to succeed. He doesn't want us to do well. He's already lost the battle for our souls. That's done. Jesus has paid it. Our works have never earned that, so God's done that. But now it's like the battle for our minds. It's the battle for us on earth and the impact we can have on earth to affect other people. So he's lost the soul, but he's going to keep on attacking your mind, because you can move powerfully if your mind's aligned and you're thinking the right thing. For example, I didn't launch my business with a Kickstarter campaign purely because, if it flopped, everyone could see. I was scared of failure. But I'm actually going to be doing one soon. I've overcome the fear.

Do you feel the challenge of balancing working crazy hard and risking doing things in your own strength and not resting so you can make time for what you need from God? Absolutely. That's a massive challenge. And that's why taking the time out to actually meditate is so important. What I've realized in my business is, there's no way on earth I could be where I am now based off my hard work. And anything that's happened that's been monumental to the business has been purely a God thing. So when I actually sit back and reflect on that, it does give me the peace of mind to try and rest more. I don't rest as much as I should and I'm driven to succeed. My motivation to succeed may not always be in the right place. But it is predominantly from a place of wanting to do well, wanting to honour God, wanting to support these children we support. But it is important to actually reflect and see that I could never have been where I am on my own.

I went to Richard Branson's house last month to discuss the business and have been backed by Virgin. No way on earth could I have done that on my own! I'm very poor with admin and long applications, and they make you do a 20- to 30-page business plan before funding. I did a four-page taster and brought it to the meeting and said, 'I'm working on the long, the real, business plan, but this just gives you an outline…' And he says, 'Oh, no, this is fine. We'll work with this.' And then, a week later, they funded me. So you look at that and you just know, it's never me.

So how did you discover the charity you support in Port Elizabeth, South Africa? It was my wife who first went out there to visit the charity about five years before we were married. The charity had been set up by one of her good friend's parents after God had spoken to them through a series of dreams. In the dreams they just kept seeing children and felt like God was saying, 'Your job is to look after them.' In another dream they saw a sign that said Brighton, and then when they were driving around South Africa on a trip they saw a sign for New Brighton in Port Elizabeth. They quit their jobs, went out there and walked into a church and told them what they were there for. One guy came up to them and said he was called to Cape Town and that they could use his house for a few months – which then turned into a few years, completely rent free! This enabled them to build the charity up and they now support over a thousand children. They give them the basic resources they need in order to go to school. So we partner with them and provide them with two sets of school uniforms, a pair of shoes and a school bag.

Tell us a bit about the first time you went out there. What were the children like? One thing I noticed about our being there was that it gave them a hope and a belief to dream. I could tell them my dad had come from circumstances just like them. And that was life-changing for me, to be able to instil that hope in these children. Afterwards you hear them saying 'I'm going to be this when I'm older…I'm going to be that' Hope is such an amazing fuel. If you've got hope, it will drive you through any adversity, because you can see light at the end of the tunnel.

And do you think that one of the core company beliefs is changing mindsets? My dream is to disrupt. I want to disrupt the watch industry and then anything I can get my hands on. And I want to disrupt it for good. I want to change the mindsets that we just buy out of self-desire.

There's nothing wrong with wanting to buy a nice watch. I'm not going to sit here and judge people for doing that. I wouldn't have any customers! But imagine a world where,

"one of my biggest passions is, especially for young black boys from the area I grew up in, giving them an example of a differe"

whenever you bought something nice and treated yourself, you could change a life in the process. I want anyone to go on my website and think, 'Wow, these products are just as good, if not better, than anyone else in the market. And when I buy one of these products, I'm impacting someone's life.' And I want to inspire people to have a mindset shift and think, even in your everyday business, what can I do that adds more purpose to what I'm doing?

Then with the children, I just want them to know they're loved. When I last went there, I met a little girl and it's mind-blowing for her to think that someone in London has woken up today and said, 'Hey, here you go, here's your school uniform.' They feel loved because people all over the world are sowing into their futures. It was important to me to support a Christian charity, even though our emphasis is on education, because I don't just want to make their lives better here on earth. A friend of mine told me off for saying that because, 'We should show love no matter what…you just showing the love is enough' – which I wholeheartedly agree with. But if I had the opportunity to show that love in an area where they're hearing about Jesus too, I'd much rather do that.

You've mentioned Richard Branson, but could you tell us about some other people who have helped you in overcoming fear and dreaming bigger? Definitely my dad. It's crazy, but I feel like my dad doesn't really see fear. When I first started the business, he was a little bit sceptical because he saw that I was earning good money and, as a loving dad, he wants what's best for me. Then he called me a week after and he said, 'Son, go for it. What you're doing is amazing.'

Wider than that, anyone who's dreamed beyond themselves is someone I look up to. Someone like Muhammad Ali or Gary Cartwright. In the world of business, a guy called Gary Vaynerchuk. His mindset is just different. When I listen to him, I feel spurred on to go on further.

Optimism is clearly a big part of your mindset. What would you say to young people who look to media and just see Brexit and terrorist attacks and unemployment? The beauty of the Bible is that it kind of clears all these things up. And there's a scripture that says, 'Faith comes by hearing.' Like, what are you feeding your soul with? What are you feeding your mind every day? If faith comes by hearing, I think fear probably comes about by hearing as well. They're both going to grow by what you feed them.And if you're constantly feeding yourself on the news, you've got to think to yourself, what mindset do these people have that are pumping this news out? Do they have my best interests at heart? Probably not. Who does have your best interests? The Word of God. It takes people like us to show them the reality of what they're spewing up and what they're saying, and show them that we actually have to be bearers of light.

Are there any particular scriptures you've held onto in times of fear? One scripture I'd say is my favourite in the Bible is Romans 12:12: 'Rejoice in hope, endure in tribulation, and persist in prayer.' I think that is the model for the Christian life. 'Rejoice in hope' – it's not saying rejoice because you have it all, but rejoice for what is to come. 'Endure in tribulation' – you're one hundred percent going to face tribulation. You're going to face hard times. But just hold on and endure. And then it all wraps up with 'persist in prayer'. So through the rejoicing, through the endurance, what's going to enable you to persist is connecting to the source, which is God – so persisting in prayer.

SO HERE'S WHAT I WANT
YOU TO DO, GOD HELPING
YOU: TAKE YOUR EVERYDAY,
ORDINARY LIFE — YOUR
SLEEPING, EATING, GOING-
TO-WORK, AND WALKING-
AROUND LIFE — AND PLACE
IT BEFORE GOD AS AN
OFFERING. EMBRACING
WHAT GOD DOES FOR YOU IS
THE BEST THING YOU CAN
DO FOR HIM. DON'T BECOME
SO WELL-ADJUSTED TO
YOUR CULTURE THAT YOU
FIT INTO IT WITHOUT EVEN
THINKING. INSTEAD, FIX
YOUR ATTENTION ON GOD.
YOU'LL BE CHANGED FROM
THE INSIDE OUT. READILY
RECOGNIZE WHAT HE
WANTS FROM YOU, AND
QUICKLY RESPOND TO IT.
UNLIKE THE CULTURE
AROUND YOU, ALWAYS
DRAGGING YOU DOWN TO
ITS LEVEL OF IMMATURITY,
GOD BRINGS THE BEST OUT
OF YOU, DEVELOPS WELL-
FORMED MATURITY IN YOU.

ROMANS 12:1-2 (MSG)

LUCILLE
HOUSTON

"By paving the way for people to understand there is so
much freedom and hope to be found in Jesus and his house.
They can find community, family and a sense of home if they
plant themselves in the house of God, the church."

> **Overcoming fear is not the absence of fear altogether, but rather feeling the fear but doing it anyway. That's definitely stuck with me.**

What's your full name?
Lucille Marguerite Houston

Where were you born?
Sydney, Australia

What do you do?
I'm a wife, a mother of four, and together with my husband we are Lead Pastors of Hillsong California.

Hobbies or things that fuel your soul? I love anything creative. Whether that is writing or dancing. Since I was a little girl, I have always loved going to watch musicals. I would go with my mom and nana growing up.

Since moving closer to the beach, it has become a go to for Ben and me. It's a place that I find instant peace and perspective. Spending time with my closest friends and family will always fuel my soul.

Who inspires you most to be fearless? The two women I look up to the most in life is my mom (Vereen Lagden) & my nana (Hilma Pristor) They have both overcome so much in their lives and yet never let anything steal their joy. They have shown me first-hand the power of putting Jesus first in your life and loving people well. They are my heroes! My kids also inspire me every day. I think I learn more from them than they learn from me. They teach me never to lose my wonder.

What were you scared of as a child? Being alone. I used to hate the feeling of being with my own thoughts too long.

What's the biggest risk you've taken?
Moving our young family halfway across the world to follow the God dream in our hearts!

Have you received any advice about overcoming fear? Overcoming fear is not the absence of fear altogether, but rather overcoming fear is feeling the fear but doing it anyway. That's definitely stuck with me.

What Key verse do you live by to overcome fear? 'But first and most importantly seek [aim at, strive after] his kingdom and his righteousness [his way of doing and being right, the attitude and character of God], and all these things will be given to you also.' Matthew 6:33.

Fear of God means that we stand in awe, in wonder, of God. What do you think is powerful and important about remembering the greatness and goodness of God? I think it's so important to be constantly reminding ourselves of God's perspective in life. His ways are higher and his thoughts are wilder than ours. Reminding ourselves of God's perfect will and timing in our lives allows us to not have to always control things. We can learn to trust God with the big things, small things and everything in between.

Trusting God is often compared to a child putting their trust in a parent. Have you learnt anything about childlike faith from your children? So much! There is something so beautiful about a child who is innocent and daring enough to dream big dreams and believe that they can do anything. My kids inspire me in that exact same way daily.

As a leader at a young and progressive church in a big city like L.A., what do you see as the biggest fear people are facing? How do you feel you and Ben are addressing it? You don't have to look very far to realize that people are living and carrying around so much fear and hurt. Whether they admit it or not, it rules people's lives, it dictates their decisions, it robs people of walking light and free in the way that God intended.

I think people want to truly feel like their hurt matters and that others see them – truly see them! Loneliness is also something that a lot of people in this city struggle with. The way we address that is by paving the way for people to understand there is so much freedom and hope to be found in Jesus and his house. They can find community, family and a sense of home if they plant themselves in the house of God, the Church.

What do you think about hope in today's culture that tells us to put our hope in things like family, relationship statuses and success? At the end of the day we all have a hole in our lives, which can only ever be truly fulfilled by a real, authentic relationship with Jesus. Until people experience that for themselves they will always try and fill that void with other things.

Was there a sense of fear when you moved to L.A. from Sydney to start the church? If so, how did you overcome it? The unknown will always come with an element of fear. But the trick is to feel the fear but do it anyway. Always trusting that if God called you he will also grace you. So just do what you can do and let him do the rest.

As a mother of four kids, what is your biggest fear in the belief system that the culture around them is promoting? That you have to be perfect or portray perfection to be liked or validated. It scares me because I want them to always know that they are enough. More than enough. They are perfect the way that God made them. Flaws and all.

What advice would you give the next generation, wanting to follow a dream but feeling fearful? I would say, do it! Feel the fear and do it anyway. I could never have imagined in my wildest dreams that I would be living on the other side of the world pastoring a multi-campus church with four kids and a big wonderful life. But here we are. And it all started with a yes and a decision to walk it out by faith even when we couldn't see what was in front of us. And we wouldn't change a thing. God is so good.

Could you tell us how you came to follow Jesus? I have always loved the house of God and grew up going to church, but it wasn't until I was sixteen that I developed my own personal revelation of what having a relationship with Jesus actually meant.

Did you feel a sense of peer pressure or a fear of rejection surrounding your relationship with Jesus? I have always had friends that don't believe in God or go to church, and I hope I always do have those friends in my life. And although some have expressed different views on things, I know that they love and respect what I believe. To be honest, when they are going through situations that are hard in their own life they often come to me for advice or help. So consistently being there for my friends is really important to me, regardless of whether we believe the same things or not.

What is the power of praise and worship, singing of God's goodness, in the face of fear? I think it shifts our perspective and focus. Instead of magnifying the fear, we magnify the Father and that changes everything.

LUCILLE HOUSTON and her husband Ben are the Lead Pastors of Hillsong Church California, with campuses in Los Angeles, Orange County, and San Francisco. They are passionate about God and the church and have a real heart to see people find hope, life and answers in Jesus Christ. They have one amazing son, Blaze, and three beautiful daughters Savannah Winter, Lexi Milan and Bailey Love.

GROUP DISCUSSION ✖ QUESTIONS
CHAPTER 6 FEAR OF GOD

As Dan sat in the prison cell at age seventeen, a dozen different fears flooded through his mind. Chief among these was the fear that, now burdened with a criminal record, he had disqualified himself from ever being used by God. However, in a moment of wisdom that belied his young age, Dan chose to turn from all his earthly fears and take on the one fear that we are called to cling to: the fear of God.

The fear of God (yes, even this has a fancy name: theophobia) is admittedly a source of disagreement, confusion and even manipulation. It has been associated with Christians cowering in terror and fleeing from the hand of a vengeful, arbitrarily judgemental God. Those who want to discredit the Christian faith have used the fear of God to justify their beliefs that Christianity is little more than a way to scare people into behaving a certain way. Regrettably, it has been used within the Church in an attempt to coerce people into following certain rules and expectations.

Is having the fear of God in us little more than being filled with sheer terror – like a mouse trapped, toyed with and ultimately killed by a predacious feline? The answer sits in a delicate tension between yes and no.

Let's be clear: our God is more than capable of striking complete terror into any one of us. The writer of Hebrews 10, when considering the fate of those who wilfully trample on God's gift of grace, concludes: 'It is a terrifying thing to fall into the hands of a living God.' God's power is awesome. His knowledge is infinite. His righteousness is beyond comprehension. His refusal to be dethroned is absolute. At the same

time, God's incredible love for us has given us the gift of life through his Son, eternally shielding us from his own wrath and judgement. The gift of his Holy Spirit can be considered a down payment on our heavenly inheritance, sealing us as his both now and forever.

Perhaps nowhere is this dichotomy articulated better than in C.S. Lewis's famed novel *The Lion, the Witch and the Wardrobe*. As a young girl draws near to a mighty lion, she muses that she hopes, for her welfare, that the lion is safe. Her guide's description of the majestic beast is telling: 'Safe? Who said anything about safe? Of course he isn't safe. But he's good. He's the king, I tell you.'

God's greatness is unparalleled, and we openly rebel against him at our own peril – but his goodness is unprecedented, and our faith in him gives us access to tremendous favour. Holding both of these ideas equally in our hearts is the key to understanding the fear of God.

REFLECTION QUESTIONS

1. Why do we typically fear God?
2. Remembering what two aspects of God's nature will help us to have a balanced, healthy fear of God?
3. Read Luke 12:4-5. Jesus recognized that there are people in our lives that can cause us to be fearful. Yet he wanted to warn us of a greater, more important fear. What was this fear? Why do you think he was giving his disciples this warning?
4. Importantly, Jesus didn't leave his disciples with a picture of a vengeful, merciless God. Continue to read Luke 12:6-7. How else does Jesus describe God? Why did Jesus strain to make this point?
5. Reflect on Mr Beaver's description of Aslan, the lion, opposite. What parallels can you draw between this king of the jungle and the King of kings?
6. Consider the multiple fears that vie to overwhelm us – the fear of failure, ridicule, rejection, loneliness and death. Now consider the fear of God. Which one is the most powerful in your life?

If the fear of God is not at the top of your list, do you think you may need to change that? If so, what would you need to do? And what would life look like when that becomes a reality for you?

BROTHERS AND SISTERS,
IN LIGHT OF ALL I HAVE SHARED
WITH YOU ABOUT GOD'S MERCIES,
I URGE YOU TO OFFER YOUR BODIES
AS A LIVING AND HOLY SACRIFICE
TO GOD, A SACRED OFFERING THAT
BRINGS HIM PLEASURE; THIS IS YOUR
REASONABLE, ESSENTIAL WORSHIP.
DO NOT ALLOW THIS WORLD TO
MOULD YOU IN ITS OWN IMAGE.
INSTEAD, BE TRANSFORMED FROM
THE INSIDE OUT BY RENEWING YOUR
MIND. AS A RESULT, YOU WILL BE ABLE
TO DISCERN WHAT GOD WILLS AND
WHATEVER GOD FINDS GOOD,
PLEASING, AND COMPLETE.

ROMANS 12:1-2 (THE VOICE)

SALVATION PRAYER

There will be many people picking up this book who don't believe in God, or who are searching for answers and exploring the Christian perspective of life. Well, if that's you, and you have got to this point and want to make a decision to follow Jesus, we'd love to help you do that. Giving your life to God really is the most powerful decision you could ever make.

The Bible says that God "desires all people to be saved and to come to the knowledge of the truth" (1 Timothy 2:4). God desires for you to accept the finished work of Jesus and give your life to him. The Bible is his love letter to you, to show you how much he cares for you and desires to be in relationship with you.

So, if you'd like to make Jesus the Lord and Saviour of your life, simply pray this prayer, wherever you are:

Heavenly Father, thank You for Your love for me and for sending Jesus to die on the cross for my sins. As I put my trust in Jesus, I am washed clean and made righteous. All my sins are forgiven. I accept your love and grace for me and ask you to be my Lord, I know that Your goodness and mercy will follow me all the days of my life from this moment on. In Jesus' name. Amen.

That decision to follow Jesus is the best you could ever make, because it has brought you into a relationship with God. By dying on a cross and rising from the dead 2000 years ago, Jesus took upon himself all the sin, shame and condemnation of humanity, giving us true freedom and eternal life.

IF YOU CONFESS WITH YOUR MOUTH THAT JESUS IS LORD AND BELIEVE IN YOUR HEART THAT GOD RAISED HIM FROM THE DEAD, YOU WILL BE SAVED. FOR WITH THE HEART ONE BELIEVES AND IS JUSTIFIED, AND WITH THE MOUTH ONE CONFESSES AND IS SAVED.
ROMANS 10:9-10 (ESV)

FEARFULLY **MADE** CONTRIBUTORS

CHAPTER ONE:
FEAR OF FAILURE
FEATURE BY: JO WATSON
UNSPLASH: JEREMY BISHOP,
ANTHONY INTRAVERSATO,
CRISTIAN NEWMAN, JESSE LEAKE

HILLSONG YOUTH   YOUNG ADULTS
- SYDNEY: DANIEL FEODOROFF
LEAD PHOTOGRAPHER: VICKI LIANG
UNSPLASH: LAURA CROS,
LUKE BENDER

INTERVIEW: FLEUR EAST
UNSPLASH: PSYCHOBALLERINA

INTERVIEW: GUVNA B
PHOTOGRAPHY: LUKE WILLIAMS
UNSPLASH: ART-BY-LONFELDT

SELAH / DISCUSSION
UNSPLASH: ARICKA LEWIS,
GABRIEL PORRAS, GHIFFARI HARIS,
TOMAS ANTON

CHAPTER TWO:
FEAR OF RIDICULE
FEATURE BY: PHIL KYEI
UNSPLASH: EVAN KRIBY,
CRISTIAN NEWMAN, GUILLE POZZI,

HILLSONG YOUTH   YOUNG ADULTS
- L.A: MARIAISABEL RODRIGUEZ
INTERVIEWER: ANGEL VASQUEZ
PHOTOGRAPHY: KEVIN VILLANUEVA
UNSPLASH: MATTHEW LEJUNE

INTERVIEW: MARCEL

INTERVIEW: LEAH McFALL

SELAH / DISCUSSION
UNSPLASH: TOBI OLUREMI,
SAMUEL ZELLER, RYAN MORENO,
CRIS DINOTO, IAN ESPINOSA,
ISWANTO ARIF, NEIL SONI,
RAFAEL ROMERO

CHAPTER THREE:
FEAR OF REJECTION
FEATURE BY: ELIZABETH NEEP
UNSPLASH: BROOKE CAGLE,
GRACE MADELINE

HILLSONG YOUTH X YOUNG ADULTS
- NYC: ANNA SOFIA VASILENKO
INTERVIEWER: RAISSA GARCIA
PHOTOGRAPHY: ERICA KIM
UNSPLASH: ANDRE BENZ

INTERVIEW:
ASHLEY JOHN-BAPTISTE
PHOTOGRAPHY: DEL MANNING
UNSPLASH: SIDHARTH BHATIA,
CLEM ONOJEGHUO

INTERVIEW: RICH WILKERSON JR
PHOTOGRAPHY: VOUS TEAM
UNSPLASH: E C CRIPPEN,
MERIC DAGLI

SELAH / DISCUSSION
UNSPLASH: CHRISTOPH SCHULZ,
FRANCESCA SARACO, NICO BHLR,
BROOKE CAGLE, MICHAEL HEUSS,
ALDAIN AUSTRIA

CHAPTER FOUR:
FEAR OF LONELINESS
FEATURE BY: ASHLEY JOHN-
BAPTISTE
UNSPLASH: ALEX IBY, ANNIE GRAY,
JAKE OATES

HILLSONG YOUTH X YOUNG ADULTS
- LONDON: JORDAN BICKNALL
PHOTOGRAPHY: LUKE WILLIAMS

INTERVIEW: CHERYL FAGAN
PHOTOGRAPHY: ELAINE KWOK
UNSPLASH: ALEX WONG, LAURA
CROS

INTERVIEW: CHELSEA SMITH
UNSPLASH: ALEX KNIGHT,
JAMES MOTTER, BLAKE LISK

SELAH / DISCUSSION
UNSPLASH: CLEM ONOJEGHUO,
OAKIE, WALL OF XAVIER,
SIEBE WARMOESKERKEN,
JACK FINNIGAN, TOMMY VAN
KESSEL, ADAM DUTTON

CHAPTER FIVE:
FEAR OF DEATH
FEATURE BY: ELIZABETH NEEP
PHOTOGRAPHY: LUKE WILLIAMS
UNSPLASH: JEREMY BISHOP,
ELTI MESHAU, TIKO GIORGADZE

TESTIMONY: CARINE HARB
PHOTOGRAPHY: LUKE WILLIAMS

INTERVIEW:
ERWIN RAPHAEL McMANUS
PHOTOGRAPHY: NICOLE LEWIS
UNSPLASH: STERLING DAVIS

SELAH / DISCUSSION
UNSPLASH: CODY SCHROEDER,
VITALY, MIGUEL PERALES,
ROBERTO NICKSON,
JOSHUA JORDAN, ALESSIO LIN,
RENEE FISHER

CHAPTER SIX:
FEAR OF GOD
FEATURE BY: DAN WATSON
UNSPLASH: ALEXANDER POPOV,
IGOR ČANČAREVIĆ, JULIEN MOREAU

HILLSONG YOUTH X YOUNG ADULTS
- PARIS: RODRIGUE VUNDILU
INTERVIEWER: LAURA CORBET
PHOTOGRAPHY: MATEUS MACHADO
UNSPLASH: PAUL GAUDRIAULT

INTERVIEW: WILLIAM ADOASI
UNSPLASH: BAN YIDO, KEVIN LEE

INTERVIEW: LUCILLE HOUSTON
PHOTOGRAPHY: JOHN POLICARPIO ,
BENTON SAMPSON
UNSPLASH: JASON LEUNG,
JOSH ROSE

SELAH / DISCUSSION
UNSPLASH: ALEX WONG, ANDRE
BENZ, DAVID SUTTON, ALEXANDER
RONSDORF, CHAD GREITER,
FLO KARR, PEDRO LASTRA, KYLO

CONTENTS PAGES
UNSPLASH: ANTHONY
INTRAVERSATO, CHRIS LIVERANI,
MING CHEN

SALVATION PRAYER
UNSPLASH: MATTHEW LEJUNE

CHAPTER COVER SHOOT &
CONTRIBUTORS
PHOTOGRAPHY: EVAN RUMMEL
(WWW.ALLSTREETS.NYC)
PHOTOGRAPHY ASSISTANT:
MICHELLE S. PALAFOX
STYLIST: KACIE PARKER
MODELS: RACHEL WATSON-JIH,
DALTON HAYS

MY IDENTITY IN JESUS
IF NOT OTHERWISE STATED THE
ANGLIZED ESV TRANSLATION

CREATIVE DIRECTOR: CARLOS DARBY
DESIGN: SUSANNA HICKLING
POST-PRODUCTION: ANDREAS SMITZ
TRANSCRIBING: LEILA JENNINGS

OH YES, YOU SHAPED ME
FIRST INSIDE, THEN OUT;
YOU FORMED ME IN MY
MOTHER'S WOMB.
I THANK YOU, HIGH GOD —
YOU'RE BREATHTAKING!
BODY AND SOUL, I AM
MARVELOUSLY MADE!
I WORSHIP IN ADORATION —
WHAT A CREATION!
YOU KNOW ME INSIDE AND OUT,
YOU KNOW EVERY BONE
IN MY BODY; YOU KNOW EXACTLY
HOW I WAS MADE, BIT BY BIT,
HOW I WAS SCULPTED FROM
NOTHING INTO SOMETHING.
LIKE AN OPEN BOOK, YOU WATCHED
ME GROW FROM CONCEPTION
TO BIRTH; ALL THE STAGES OF
MY LIFE WERE SPREAD OUT
BEFORE YOU, THE DAYS OF MY LIFE
ALL PREPARED BEFORE I'D EVEN
LIVED ONE DAY.

PSALM 139:13-16 (MSG)

THANK YOU

Hillsong Youth & Young Adults for generously contributing to this book and to all the people behind the scenes that made this book possible. To Tricia Hidalgo, Mariana Arteaga, Christy Adams, Alisah Duran, Christy Adams, Joey Miranda and Elizabeth Neep - your patience and assistance were invaluable. To the Unsplash community for their generosity in providing photography.

HILLSONG YOUTH & YOUNG ADULTS

Hillsong is a large Bible-based, Christ-centred church which now has churches in city centres in 21 countries around the world. Hillsong London meets in various locations across the city and has a fast-growing youth ministry, Hillsong Youth and Young Adults. This ministry is all about engaging this age group with the words and works of Jesus and empowering each of them to believe they can positively shape society.
@HILLSONGYXYA

ABRUPT MEDIA

Our passion is to inspire a visual generation by creating dynamic resources for individuals who are seeking to understand the truth of the gospel.

www.abrupt-media.com and @ABRUPTMEDIA

I AM THE AROMA OF CHRIST [2 Corinthians 2:15] – For we are the aroma of Christ to God among those who are being saved and among those who are perishing. I AM NOT ASHAMED [2 Timothy 1:12 (NIV)] That is why I am suffering as I am. Yet this is no cause for shame, because I know whom I have believed, and am convinced that he is able to guard what I have entrusted to him until that day. I AM ASSURED OF REWARD [1 Corinthians 15:58 (NIV)] Therefore, my dear brothers and sisters, stand firm. Let nothing move you. Always give yourselves fully to the work of the Lord, because you know that your labour in the Lord is not in vain. I AM BECOMING A MATURE PERSON [Ephesians 4:13 (NIV)] – Until we all reach unity in the faith and in the knowledge of the Son of God and become mature, attaining to the whole measure of the fullness of Christ. I AM BECOMING CONFORMED TO CHRIST [Romans 8:29] – For those whom he foreknew he also predestined to be conformed to the image of his Son, in order that he might be the firstborn among many brothers. I AM A BELIEVER [Romans 10:9 (NIV)] If you declare with your mouth, "Jesus is Lord," and believe in your heart that God raised him from the dead, you will be saved. I AM ENRICHED IN EVERYTHING [1 Corinthians 1:5 (NIV)] – For in him you have been enriched in every way – with all kinds of speech and with all knowledge. I AM EQUIPPED [2 Timothy 3:16-17] – All Scripture is breathed out by God and profitable for teaching, for reproof, for correction, and for training in righteousness, that the man of God may be competent, equipped for every good work. I AM INSEPARABLE FROM HIS LOVE [Romans 8:35] – Who shall separate us from the love of Christ? Shall tribulation, or distress, or persecution, or famine, or nakedness, or danger, or sword? I AM A CHILD OF GOD [John 1:12-13] – But to all who did receive him, who believed in his name, he gave the right to become children of God, who were born, not of blood nor of the will of the flesh nor of the will of man, but of God. I AM CHERISHED [Ephesians 5:29-30] For no one ever hated his own flesh, but nourishes and cherishes it, just as Christ does the Church, because we are members of his body. I AM CONFIDENT OF ANSWERS TO PRAYERS [1 John 5:14-15] – And this is the confidence that we have towards him, that if we ask anything according to his will he hears us. And if we know that he hears us in whatever we ask, we know that we have the requests that we have asked of him. I AM A CONQUEROR [Romans 8:37] – No, in all these things we are more than conquerors through him who loved us. I AM FAITHFUL [Revelation 17:14 (NIV)] – They will wage war against the Lamb, but the Lamb will triumph over them because he is Lord of lords and King of kings – and with him will be his called, chosen and faithful followers. I AM FAMILY [Psalm 68:5-6 (TPT)] – To the fatherless he is a father. To the widow he is a champion friend. To the lonely he gives a family. To the prisoners he leads into prosperity until they sing for joy. This is our Holy God in his Holy Place! But for the rebels there is heartache and despair. I AM FAR FROM OPPRESSION [Isaiah 54:14] – In righteousness you shall be established; you shall be far from oppression, for you shall not fear; and from terror, for it shall not come near you. I AM HIS BROTHER [Hebrew 2:11 (NIV)] Both the one who makes people holy and those who are made holy are of the same family. So Jesus is not ashamed to call them brothers and sisters. I AM BROUGHT NEAR [Ephesians 2:13] – But now in Christ Jesus you who once were far off have been brought near by the blood of Christ. I AM GRANTED GRACE IN CHRIST JESUS [Romans 5:17] – For if, because of one man's trespass, death reigned through that one man, much more will those who receive the abundance of grace and the free gift of righteousness reign in life through the one man Jesus Christ. I AM JUSTIFIED [Acts 13:39 (NIV)] – Through him everyone who believes is set free from every sin, a justification you were not able to obtain under the law of Moses. I AM KEPT [Isaiah 38:17] – Surely it was for my benefit that I suffered such anguish. In your love you kept me from the pit of destruction; you have put all my sins behind your back. I AM HOLY [Ephesians 1:4] – Even as he chose us in him before the foundation of the world, that we should be holy and blameless before him. I AM HONOURED [2 Timothy 2:21] – Therefore, if anyone cleanses himself from what is dishonourable, he will be a vessel for honourable use, set apart as holy, useful to the master of the house, ready for every good work. I AM LED IN CHRIST'S TRIUMPH [2 Corinthians 2:14] – But thanks be to God, who in Christ always leads us in triumphal procession, and through us spreads the fragrance of the knowledge of him everywhere. I AM LIBERATED [Romans 6:23] – For the wages of sin is death, but the free gift of God is eternal life in Christ Jesus our Lord. I AM LOVED [John 3:16] – For God so loved the world, that he gave his only Son, that whoever believes in him should not perish but have eternal life. I AM GOD'S GIFT TO CHRIST [John 17:24] – Father, I desire that they also, whom you have given me, may be with me where I am, to see my glory that you have given me because you loved me before the foundation of the world. I AM GLORIFIED WITH HIM [2 Thessalonians 2:14 (NIV)] – He called you to this through our gospel, that you might share in the glory of our Lord Jesus Christ. I AM LIGHT IN A DARK PLACE [Acts 13:47] – For so the Lord has commanded us, saying, "I have made you a light for the Gentiles, that you may bring salvation to the ends of the earth." I AM A LIVING STONE IN A SPIRITUAL HOUSE [1 Peter 2:5] – You yourselves like living stones are being built up as a spiritual house, to be a holy priesthood, to offer spiritual sacrifices acceptable to God through Jesus Christ. I AM CARED FOR [1 Peter 5:7 (NIV)] – Cast all your anxiety on him because he cares for you. I AM CARRIED [Exodus 19:4 (NIV)] – You yourselves have seen what I did to Egypt, and how I carried you on eagles' wings and brought you to myself. I AM FILLED [Acts 2:4] And they were all filled with the Holy Spirit and began to speak in other tongues as the Spirit gave them utterance. I AM FILLED TO THE FULLNESS OF GOD [Colossians 2:9-10] – For in him the whole fullness of deity dwells bodily, and you have been filled in him, who is the head of all rule and authority. I AM FILLED WITH THE FRUIT OF RIGHTEOUSNESS [Philippians 1:11] – Filled with the fruit of righteousness that comes through Jesus Christ, to the glory and praise of God. I AM FAVOURED [Job 10:12] - You have granted me life and steadfast love, and your care has preserved my spirit. I AM A CITIZEN WITH THE SAINTS [Ephesians 2:19] - So then you are no longer strangers and aliens, but you are fellow citizens with the saints and members of the household of God I AM CHOSEN [1 Peter 2:9] - But you are a chosen race, a royal priesthood, a holy nation, a people for his own possession, that you may proclaim the excellencies of him who called you out of darkness into his marvellous light. I AM A CITIZEN OF HEAVEN [Philippians 3:20-21 (NIV)] - But our citizenship is in heaven. And we eagerly await a Savior from there, the Lord Jesus Christ, who, by the power that enables him to bring everything under his control, will transform our lowly bodies so that they will be like his glorious body. I AM ABOUNDING IN GRACE [2 Corinthians 9:8] - And God is able to make all grace abound to you, so that having all sufficiency in all things at all times, you may abound in every good work. I AM BEAUTIFUL [Psalm 149:4] - For the Lord takes pleasure in his people; he adorns the humble with salvation.

MY IDENTITY IN JESUS